UBICOMM 2020

The Fourteenth International Conference on Mobile Ubiquitous Computing, Systems, Services and Technologies

October 25 - 29, 2020

UBICOMM 2020 Editors

Cosmin Dini, IARIA EU/USA

Dmitry Korzun, Petrozavodsk State University, Russia

Printed from e-media with permission by:

Curran Associates, Inc.
57 Morehouse Lane
Red Hook, NY 12571

International Academy, Research, and Industry Association (IARIA)
412 Derby Way
Wilmington, DE 19810

Phone: (408) 893-6407
Fax: (408) 527-6351

petre@iaria.org

Additional copies of this publication are available from:

Curran Associates, Inc.
57 Morehouse Lane
Red Hook, NY 12571 USA
Phone: 845-758-0400
Fax: 845-758-2633
Email: curran@proceedings.com
Web: www.proceedings.com

Table of Contents

UBICOMM 2020

Forward

The Fourteenth International Conference on Mobile Ubiquitous Computing, Systems, Services and Technologies (UBICOMM 2020), held on October 22-29, 2020, continued a series of evens meant to bring together researchers from the academia and practitioners from the industry in order to address fundamentals of ubiquitous systems and the new applications related to them.

The rapid advances in ubiquitous technologies make fruition of more than 35 years of research in distributed computing systems, and more than two decades of mobile computing. The ubiquity vision is becoming a reality. Hardware and software components evolved to deliver functionality under failure-prone environments with limited resources. The advent of web services and the progress on wearable devices, ambient components, user-generated content, mobile communications, and new business models generated new applications and services. The conference makes a bridge between issues with software and hardware challenges through mobile communications.

Advances in web services technologies along with their integration into mobility, online and new business models provide a technical infrastructure that enables the progress of mobile services and applications. These include dynamic and on-demand service, context-aware services, and mobile web services. While driving new business models and new online services, particular techniques must be developed for web service composition, web service-driven system design methodology, creation of web services, and on-demand web services.

As mobile and ubiquitous computing becomes a reality, more formal and informal learning will take pace out of the confines of the traditional classroom. Two trends converge to make this possible; increasingly powerful cell phones and PDAs, and improved access to wireless broadband. At the same time, due to the increasing complexity, modern learners will need tools that operate in an intuitive manner and are flexibly integrated in the surrounding learning environment.

Educational services will become more customized and personalized, and more frequently subjected to changes. Learning and teaching are now becoming less tied to physical locations, co-located members of a group, and co-presence in time. Learning and teaching increasingly take place in fluid combinations of virtual and "real" contexts, and fluid combinations of presence in time, space and participation in community. To the learner full access and abundance in communicative opportunities and information retrieval represents new challenges and affordances. Consequently, the educational challenges are numerous in the intersection of technology development, curriculum development, content development and educational infrastructure.

The conference had the following tracks:

- Ubiquitous software and security
- Ubiquitous networks
- Fundamentals

- Users, applications, and business models
- Ubiquity trends and challenges

We take here the opportunity to warmly thank all the members of the UBICOMM 2020 technical program committee, as well as all the reviewers. The creation of such a high quality conference program would not have been possible without their involvement. We also kindly thank all the authors that dedicated much of their time and effort to contribute to UBICOMM 2020. We truly believe that, thanks to all these efforts, the final conference program consisted of top quality contributions.

We also gratefully thank the members of the UBICOMM 2020 organizing committee for their help in handling the logistics and for their work that made this professional meeting a success.

We hope that UBICOMM 2020 was a successful international forum for the exchange of ideas and results between academia and industry and to promote further progress in the field of mobile ubiquitous computing, systems, services and technologies.

UBICOMM 2020 General Chair

Jaime Lloret Mauri, Polytechnic University of Valencia, Spain

UBICOMM 2020 Steering Committee

Wladyslaw Homenda, Warsaw University of Technology, Poland
Vitaly Klyuev, University of Aizu, Japan

UBICOMM 2020 Publicity Chair

Daniel Andoni Basterrechea, Universitat Politecnica de Valencia, Spain

UBICOMM 2020

COMMITTEE

UBICOMM 2020 General Chair

Jaime Lloret Mauri, Polytechnic University of Valencia, Spain

UBICOMM Steering Committee

Wladyslaw Homenda, Warsaw University of Technology, Poland
Vitaly Klyuev, University of Aizu, Japan

UBICOMM 2020 Publicity Chair

Daniel Andoni Basterrechea, Universitat Politecnica de Valencia, Spain

UBICOMM 2020 Technical Program Committee

Afrand Agah, West Chester University of Pennsylvania, USA
Wafaa Ait-Cheik-Bihi, Itris Automation by Schneider Electric, France
A. B. M. Alim Al Islam, Bangladesh University of Engineering and Technology, Bangladesh
Sadam Al-Azani, King Fahd University of Petroleum and Minerals (KFUPM), Saudi Arabia
Mrim Alnfiai, Dalhousie University, Canada
Tahssin Altabbaa, Istanbul Gelisim University / Huawei Istanbul, Turkey
Mohsen Amini Salehi, University of Louisiana at Lafayette, USA
Nafisa Anzum, University of Waterloo, Canada
Mehran Asadi, Lincoln University, USA
F. Mzee Awuor, Kisii University, Kenya
Muhammed Ali Aydin, Istanbul University - Cerrahpasa, Turkey
Matthias Baldauf, FHS St.Gallen, Switzerland
Oladayo Bello, Johns Hopkins University, USA
Imed Ben Dhaou, University of Turku, Finland
Djamal Benslimane, Université Claude Bernard Lyon 1, France
Aurelio Bermúdez, Universidad de Castilla-La Mancha, Spain
Nik Bessis, Edge Hill University, UK
Robert Bestak, Czech Technical University in Prague, Czech Republic
Sourav Kumar Bhoi, Parala Maharaja Engineering College, India
Azedine Boulmakoul, Université Hassan II de Casablanca, Morocco
Lars Braubach, Complex Software Systems | Bremen City University, Germany
Christian Cabrera, Trinity College Dublin, Ireland
João Carreira, Instituto de Telecomunicações, Portugal
Chao Chen, Purdue University Fort Wayne, USA
Michael Collins, Technological University Dublin, Ireland
André Constantino da Silva, IFSP & NIED/UNICAMP, Brazil
Roland Dodd, Central Queensland University, Australia
Ivanna Dronyuk, Lviv Polytechnic National University, Ukraine

Francisco Falcone, ISC-UPNA, Spain
Andras Farago, University of Texas at Dallas, USA
Olga Fedevych, Lviv Polytechnic National University, Ukraine
Renato Ferrero, Politecnico di Torino, Italy
Olivier Flauzac, University of Reims, France
Franco Frattolillo, University of Sannio, Benevento, Italy
Stéphane Galland, Belfort-Montbéliard University of Technology, France
Crescenzio Gallo, University of Foggia, Italy
Chris Gniady, University of Arizona, USA
Ann Gordon-Ross, University of Florida, USA
Weixi Gu, UCBerkeley, USA
Qiang (Nathan) He, Swinburne University of Technology, Australia
Wladyslaw Homenda, Warsaw University of Technology, Poland
Tzung-Pei Hong, National University of Kaohsiung, Taiwan
Yasser Ismail, Southern University and A&M College, USA
Jacek Izydorczyk, Instytut Elektroniki Politechniki Śląskiej, Gliwice, Poland
Mehmet Karakoç, Alanya Hamdullah Emin Paşa University - Antalya, Turkey
Reinhard Klemm, Avaya Labs, USA
Vitaly Klyuev, University of Aizu, Japan
Dmitry Korzun, Petrozavodsk State University, Russia
Konstantinos Kotis, University of the Aegean, Greece
Pierre Leone, University of Geneva, Switzerland
Mauro Henrique Lima de Boni, Federal Institute of Education, Science and Technology of Tocantins - IFTO, Brazil
Jianqing Liu, University of Alabama in Huntsville, USA
Xiaodong Liu, Edinburgh Napier University, UK
Xiaoli Liu, University of Helsinki, Finland
Jaime Lloret Mauri, Polytechnic University of Valencia, Spain
Giuseppe Loseto, Polytechnic University of Bari, Italy
Aliane Loureiro Krassmann, Federal Institute Farroupilha, Brazil
Derdour Makhlouf, University of Tebessa, Algeria
Sathiamoorthy Manoharan, University of Auckland, New Zealand
Josep Maria Salanova Grau, Center for Research and Technology Hellas, Greece
Francesca Martelli, Istituto di Informatica e Telematica (CNR), Italy
Abdul-Rahman Mawlood-Yunis, Wilfrid Laurier University, Waterloo, Canada
Weizhi Meng, Technical University of Denmark, Denmark
Philippe Merle, Inria Lille - Nord Europe, France
Daniela Micucci, University of Milano - Bicocca, Italy
Habib Mostafaei, Universität Berlin, Germany
Mjumo Mzyece, University of the Witwatersrand, Johannesburg, South Africa
Ryo Nishide, Shiga University, Japan
Kouzou Ohara, Aoyama Gakuin University, Japan
Satoru Ohta, Toyama Prefectural University, Japan
K. K. Pattanaik, ABV-Indian Institute of Information Technology and Management, Gwalior, India
Elena Renda, IIT - CNR, Italy
André Restivo, University of Porto, Portugal
Vanlin Robinson, University of Chicago, USA
Michele Ruta, Politecnico di Bari, Italy

Copyright Information

Fault Diagnosis for Industrial Rotary Machinery based on Edge Computing and Neural Networking

Valentin Perminov*, Vladislav Ermakov*, Dmitry Korzun*
* Petrozavodsk State University (PetrSU), Petrozavodsk, Russia
Email: perminov@cs.petrsu.ru, vlaermak@cs.petrsu.ru, dkorzun@cs.karelia.ru

***Abstract*—Recent progress in Sensorics and Internet of Things (IoT) enables real-time data analytics based on data from multiple sensors covering the target industrial production system and its manufacturing processes. Diagnostics and prognosis can be implemented using the neural network approach on top of vibration and other sensed data. Neural network methods lead to high accuracy in fault detection and fault evolution. Nevertheless, transferring a neural network model to edge devices leads to performance issues and platform limitations. In this paper, we discuss the edge computing opportunities for diagnostics of industrial rotary machinery using well-known neural network methods.**

Keywords–Fault diagnosis; convolutional neural network; edge computing; vibration diagnostics.

I. INTRODUCTION

The recent progress in Sensorics and Internet of Things (IoT) enables real-time data analytics for industrial systems [1]. The analytics—diagnostics and prognosis—is based on data coming in from multiple sensors [2] (i.e., multi-parametric monitoring). Many sensors cover the target industrial production system to monitor its technical state, utilization conditions, and underlying manufacturing processes.

In this paper, we focus on the fault diagnostics problem for industrial rotary machinery. Mechanical parts (e.g., rolling bearings and electric motor rotors) are monitored in real-time [3]. First, we study the problem of applying the Convolutional Neural Network (CNN) methods to detect faults and to evaluate fault characteristics [4]. Second, we study how low-capacity edge IoT devices can be useful to perform data analysis in real-time [5].

Diagnostics and prognosis can be implemented using the CNN methods on top of vibration and other sensed data [6]. The CNN methods lead to high accuracy in fault detection and evaluation [7]. The topical practical problem in industrial rotary machinery fault diagnosis is bearing fault detection. The diagnostics could be done by analysis of vibration data from sensors installed at the unit under monitoring. We consider the case when a CNN is applied for bearing fault classification, based on raw vibration signal analysis.

To obtain diagnostics results in real-time the network latency and traffic volume should be reduced in transferring data to the processing center. Data processing must be implemented near the machinery in real-time. We consider an industrial monitoring system with edge CNN computing devices. Flow data from the sensors go to an edge CNN computing device either directly through wired/wireless interfaces or through aggregator IoT devices. Deploying a CNN model to edge devices has platform limitations and leads to the performance issues. We experiment with the performance estimation of such edge device. We show that low-capacity edge IoT devices have enough performance to make data analysis based on CNN in industrial monitoring tasks.

The rest of the paper is organized as follows. Section II considers existing approaches to rotating machinery fault diagnosis: Condition Monitoring (CM) and Prognostic Health Monitoring (PHM). Section III defines the problem of vibration diagnostics in rotary machinery. Section IV shows the possible methods to solve the problem of vibration diagnostics in rotary machinery. Section V presents positive results of our feasibility study on the applicability. Section VI summarizes the results of this study.

II. RELATED WORK

There are two approaches to rotating machinery fault diagnosis: CM and PHM.

The first technique is a condition monitoring using feature extraction from the raw signal. In the study [3], there is a method for CM based on feature extraction from the raw signal. The raw signal is divided into frames, and the set of features from each frame is extracted. The feature set for each frame includes time, frequency, and time-frequency domain features. The extracted features are used for machine learning algorithms to classify the rolling bearing condition state.

In [8] Remaining Useful Life (RUL) criterion is proposed to estimate bearing condition in the future. The proposed method includes filtering the raw signals using Discrete Wavelet Transform (DWT), then extracting time, frequency, and time-frequency domain features. An autoregressive model is then established for each of the extracted features. The optimum features are then selected using a kernel-based Extreme Learning Machine (ELM) algorithm and Performance Evaluation Criterion (PEC). In the training stage of the method, the selected features are used as inputs to the PHM algorithm, while the RUL is used as the target vector. A degradation model is obtained after the training stage, which is used together with the testing input features to predict the fractional RUL of the test data.

Another approach is a raw signal analysis using Deep Learning (DL) algorithms. In [6], CNN is used to evaluate the rolling bearing fault type. The vibration signal presented as a vector of N-samples is selected as an input for CNN. Plenty of convolution layers extracts features from the raw signal that is analyzed by fully-connected layers. The output of the proposed model presents an M-length vector, where M — is the number of condition states. Additionally, data fusing is applied to evaluate more performance from the proposed method. In this case, the input data presented as a set of vectors: vibration signal vector, and two-phase motor current vector, that spins the shaft with installed bearing.

Palossi et al. demonstrated a navigation engine for autonomous nano-drones capable of closed-loop end-to-end

CNN-based visual navigation [9]. They deployed DroNet neural network to the GAP8 processor and achieved power consumption of CNN processing of only 64 mW on average.

In [10], a real-time fault detection system called LiReD was implemented for an industrial robot manipulator. The system consisted of a Raspberry Pi single-board computer and a piezo-electric accelerometer. The Long Short-Term Memory (LSTM) recurrent neural network was used to analyze the vibration signal with the aim of vacuum ejector fault detection. The LSTM-based fault detection model was compared with k-Nearest Neighbor with Dynamic Time Warping (k-NN+DTW), Random Forest (RF), and Support Vector Machine (SVM). The LSTM-based fault detection model showed the best performance, among others. The authors note that more complex analysis and more complex neural networks will require more efficient hardware, and retraining and compression techniques that reduce the size of the model but increase or maintain its performance.

III. Vibration Diagnostics in Rotary Machinery

To keep industrial machinery in appropriate condition, the methods of technical condition monitoring (diagnostics) and predictive maintenance are applied. The diagnostics are based on the current machinery state by obtaining signals from various sensors. The predictive maintenance aims at forecasting behavior mechanisms at a certain point in time with the current state. Both of these methods found application in the Industrial Internet of Things (IIoT) diagnostic systems. The utilization of condition diagnostics and predictive maintenance services establishes an effective equipment machinery operation mode and personnel timetable.

A. Condition monitoring for rolling bearing

Rotary machinery and their mechanical parts, such as bearings and electric motor rotors, must be monitored online. CM with offline-based systems performs post-processing operations on a remote server. Hence the results of the diagnostics could not be obtained instantly. To get this result near the machinery online, the special methods and hardware should be applied. This possibility could be obtained by using edge computing devices. These devices are portable apparatus installed near the machinery for online condition diagnostics. The raw data from various sensors, installed on an object, are collected by the edge device for analysis. The flow-based data, in case of continuous sensing and processing of different data types, are performed for:

- mechanical parts vibration, position, speed;
- electric motor current;
- temperature;
- acoustic signals.

The methods need to analyze data from various sensors by applying special techniques to increase performance on an edge computing device. Especially for bearings, the condition state could be obtained by a vibration signal analysis. Some approaches include envelope spectrum analysis with Fast Fourier Transform (FFT) and neural network methods with feature extraction. The vibration signal and its spectrum includes the most important information about bearing condition state. For example, the vibration signal, in case of inner ring defect, presents a normal noise, modulated by hight order rotary speed harmonics. When developing a mobile device for CM, the selected hardware must provide an effective implementation of the diagnostic method through the use of dedicated hardware processing units, such as Digital Signal Processing (DSP) unit and neural network accelerator. Hence, in this work, edge computing opportunities were applied to rolling bearing diagnosticians with the proposed model based on CNN.

B. The dataset description

The big dataset should be used to train a CNN. For online condition diagnostic, it is important to know a bearing state: "healthy" or "damaged". The causes and types of damages could be studied with server-class computers. To evaluate the applied model performance, the Paderborn University Bearing Dataset was selected as a dataset for train and test data [3]. The dataset consists of MatLab files with measurements from various sensors, such as accelerometer, current sensor, torque sensor, and thermometer. The experimental dataset was obtained using a specific test rig, see Figure 1, which was designed and operated at the Chair of Design and Drive Technology, Paderborn University.

The test rig is a modular system to ensure the flexible use of different defects in an electrically driven mechanical drive train. The test rig consists of several modules: an electric motor (1), a torque-measurement shaft (2), a rolling bearing test module (3), a flywheel (4), and a load motor (5).

The ball bearings with different types of damage are mounted in the bearing test module to generate the experimental data. For the generation of the measurement data, the current signals of the electric motor are recorded. The vibration and current signal were measured with a 64 kHz sample rate under different conditions for 32 bearings with four-digit code.

The dataset provides four types of bearings, described in Table I: "healthy" – with no damages, "IR" – inner ring defect, "OR" – outer ring defect, "IR+OR" – both inner and outer ring defects.

TABLE I. The dataset bearings.

Healthy	*"IR"*	*"OR"*	*"IR+OR"*
K001	KA01	KI01	KB23
K002	KA03	KI03	KB24
K003	KA04	KI04	KB27
K004	KA05	KI05	
K005	KA06	KI07	
K006	KA07	KI08	
	KA08	KI14	
	KA09	KI16	
	KA15	KI17	
	KA16	KI18	
	KA22	KI21	
	KA30		

According to the nature of the defect, damaged bearings belong to two main groups, which are described in Table II: artificially damaged bearings and bearings with real damages. Artificial damages were made by electric discharge machining, drilling, and manual electric engraving with a different extent. Real damages were generated by accelerated lifetime tests.

Each bearing used to run under different speed, torque and radial load — 20 measurements of 4 seconds each for each operating condition, saved as a MatLab file (80 in total) with a name consisting of the code of the operating condition and the four-digit, bearing code (e.g., N15_M07_F10_KA01_1.mat).

IV. Edge-Centric Neural Network Computing

In this section, we suggest the concept of an industrial monitoring system and describe its prototype used in this

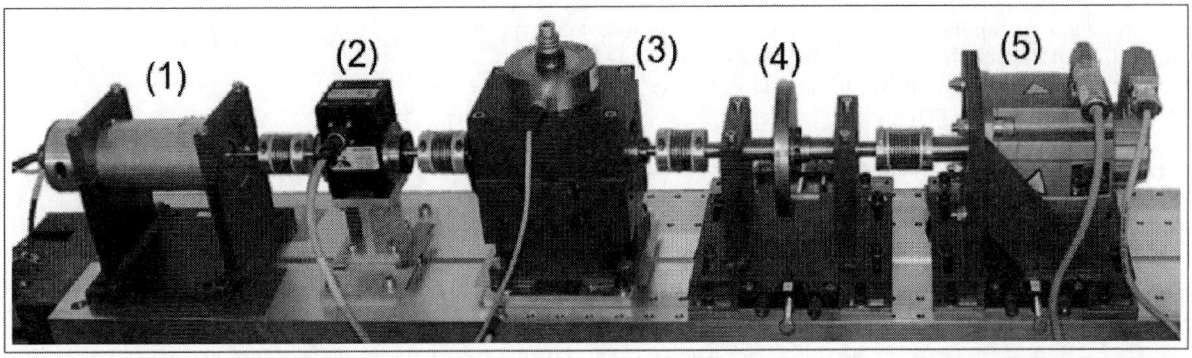

Figure 1. Test rig setup: (1) – electric motor, (2) – torque-measurement shaft, (3) – rolling bearing test module, (4) – flywheel, (5) – load motor [3].

TABLE II. DAMAGED BEARINGS TYPES.

Artificially damaged	*With real damages*
KA01	KA04
KA03	KA15
KA05	KA16
KA06	KA22
KA07	KA30
KA08	KB23
KA09	KB24
KI01	KB27
KI03	KI04
KI05	KI14
KI07	KI16
KI08	KI17
	KI18
	KI21

paper. Also, we provide a description of CNN for bearings fault detection, training and validation datasets, and used software tools and frameworks.

A. Edge-Centric Neural Network Computing Device

The rotating machinery fault diagnosis as a part of the industrial monitoring system could extract information from various sensors to make desitions about technical condition of equipment. Such sensors could be accelerometers, encoders, thermosensors, current and acoustic sensors. The data from sensors could flow to neural network computing device directly through wired or wireless interfaces or through aggregation devices. In our experiment, we simulate dataflow from sensors by a personal computer reading files from bearing vibration signal dataset and send frames of this signal via Universal Asynchronous Receiver-Transmitter (UART) to the neural network computing device. As such a device, we use Kendryte K210 system-on-chip, which has build-in dual-core Central Processing Unit (CPU) to execute a control algorithm, peripheral interfaces to interact with different sensors and communication modules, including digital accelerometers and wireless adapters, and CNN hardware accelerator unit designed for efficient CNN inference [11]. These properties make it well suited for IoT applications. And as we show in Section V, its performance enough for edge-centric rotating machinery fault diagnosis. However, this device has the next limitations that should be considered during application development. First, the built-in static random access memory (SRAM) is limited down to 8 MB, two of which are dedicated to the CNN accelerator. This means that neural network runtime data must not exceed 2 MB and executable code of control algorithm along with neural network weights should not exceed 6 MB. For sequential CNN, the runtime data could be estimated as a maximum sum of feature maps of two sequential layers. Second, as this device designed to be low-power and mobile, its performance is restricted, and standard CPU frequency is reduced down to 400 MHz. To reach maximum performance, most of the operations should be expressed through convolution to be processed by the CNN hardware accelerator.

Below we describe CNN developed to perform rotating machinery fault diagnosis running on the edge neural network computing device.

B. CNN for vibration signal based bearings fault detection

In this paper, we use the CNN for vibration signal based bearings fault detection. The input data of purposed CNN is raw vibration signal from the accelerometer installed close to the bearing. The CNN is composed of the sequence of three 1-D convolutional and pooling layers, followed by two fully-connected layers. The last layer consists of three nodes, corresponding to three detected classes: healthy bearing, damage of the outer ring, and damage of the inner ring. The concept of application of CNN to vibration signal classification, as a special case of time series classification, consists of follows.

The first convolutional layer applies multiple filters to the input 1-D tensor. Each filter has an individual convolution kernel for each channel of the input tensor. As the input of the first layer is only a vibration signal, input tensor has only one channel, so each filter has one kernel and applies one convolution to the input tensor. As there are multiple filters in the layer, this produces multiple outputs. In the case of a 2-D convolutional layer applied to spatial data (such as an image), the outputs are also is two-dimensional and represent spatial feature distribution, so the set of these outputs is referred to as a feature map, where each channel corresponds to the certain feature. In the case of raw vibration signal processing, we convolve signal (1-D vector) along the time axis by 1-D convolutions and obtain a set of 1-D vectors represented time distribution of features. We will refer to this set as a feature map and distinguish individual 1-D vector as a channel, to preserve common terminology.

Each convolution could be treated as filtering, or as a cross-correlation between raw signal and certain pattern. The form of filter kernel or cross-correlation pattern is defined during the training process. This allows CNN to automatically learn and extract features that best describe the data.

After the convolutional layer, the pooling layer is applied.

It performs down-sampling of the feature map. We use max-pooling for all layers. It allows us to preserve the most important information and significantly reduce feature map size and computation amount.

The next two couple of convolutional and max-pooling layers performs extraction features of an ever-higher level of abstraction. Finally, the last two fully-connected layers perform classification based on the extracted features.

The hyperparameters of CNN, such as the number of layers, number of units in fully-connected layers, number of filters and size of kernels in convolutional layers, have been selected through manual search and tuning with the aim to maximize accuracy on the validation set and prevent the overfitting.

The input of CNN is the 1-D tensor of 8192 samples of normalized vibration signal recorded at 64 kHz sample rate, which equals to 128 ms. Considering that the lowest rotation speed is 900 rpm, the full revolution takes approximately 67 ms or less. Thus, 128 ms should be sufficient to detect distinctive vibration produced by defects. The output of CNN is the 1-D tensor of three elements corresponded to the probabilities of detected classes. To train CNN we use Adam optimizer [12] with learning rate 0.00001 and categorical cross-entropy loss function. The number of training epoch is determined during the training process by monitoring the validation loss and when it has stopped decreasing the training process is terminated. The detailed description of used CNN is shown in Table III.

TABLE III. DESCRIPTION OF CNN HYPERPARAMETERS.

Layer	*Shape*	*Parameters*	
Input	(8192)		
1D Convolutional Layer	(8192, 2)	Activation	ReLU
		Filters	2
		Kernel Size	64
		Stride	1
		Padding	Same
1D Pooling Layer	(512, 2)	Pool size	16
1D Convolutional Layer	(512, 12)	Activation	ReLU
		Filters	12
		Kernel Size	32
		Stride	1
		Padding	Same
1D Pooling Layer	(32, 12)	Pool size	16
1D Convolutional Layer	(32, 32)	Activation	ReLU
		Filters	32
		Kernel Size	16
		Stride	1
		Padding	Same
1D Pooling Layer	(2, 32)	Pool size	16
Fully-connected layer	(150)	Activation	Sigmoid
		Units	150
Fully-connected layer	(3)	Activation	Softmax
		Units	3

For the training and evaluation of CNN, we use Paderborn University Dataset [3]. We select five bearings for each class. For outer ring damage and inner ring damage classes, the bearings with real damages have been chosen. The categorization of the dataset is given in Table IV. On the basis that, in the practical application, the monitored physical objects (bearings) differ from ones used in the training process, the validation split has been made by bearing's name rather than random examples splitting. We split the dataset into two parts: training set (set 2-5 in Table IV) and validation set (set 1 in Table IV). As recorded signal length in each file in the used dataset is 4 seconds, but CNN input length is 128 ms, at each training step a random frame of 128 ms is selected from random file from the dataset.

TABLE IV. CATEGORIZATION OF DATASET.

Set No.	*Healthy (Class 1)*	*Outer ring damage (Class 2)*	*Inner ring damage (Class 3)*
1	K001	KA04	KI04
2	K002	KA15	KI14
3	K003	KA16	KI16
4	K004	KA22	KI18
5	K005	KA30	KI21

To implement CNN, we use Keras with TensorFlow backend. To deploy CNN to Kendryte K210 system-on-chip, we convert our CNN to the TensorFlow Lite FlatBuffer file (.tflite) [13], and next, we compile it by nncase utility [14] to KModel format, which could be executed on the Kendryte K210 with hardware acceleration of convolution.

V. FEASIBILITY STUDY

In this section, to test the applicability of proposed CNN for bearings fault detection and classification, we train and test on Paderborn University Bearing Dataset [3]. We analyze obtained learning curves and confusion matrices. To test the portability of proposed CNN to edge devices, we deploy trained CNN to Kendryte K210 system-on-chip and evaluate its performance.

A. CNN training and testing

The set of training trials with fixed hyperparameters and random weights initialization has been conducted and the best one had been selected. The learning curves of CNN accuracy and loss on the training and validation datasets are shown in Figures 2 and 3. The result shows that after approximately 60 training epochs the validation loss is steady at the same level, so the training process had been terminated. The validation accuracy steady at 88%.

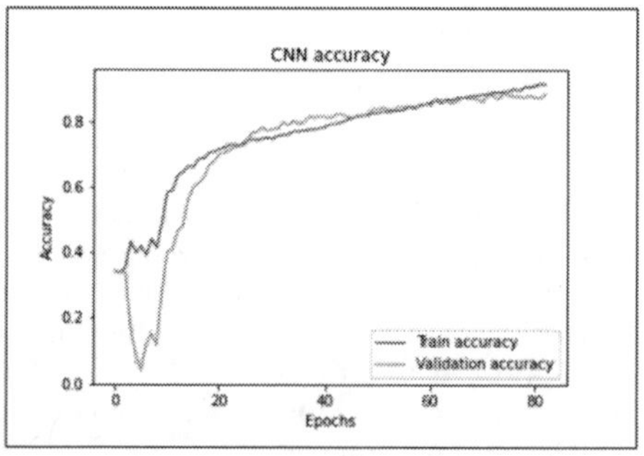

Figure 2. Training and validation accuracy curves of CNN.

The confusion matrices on training and validation data are shown in Figures 4 and 5, respectively. It could be noticed that obtained CNN shows the high classification accuracy both on training and validation data. This result allows us to use CNN not only for fault detection tasks, but also for determine the fault type.

B. CNN performance evaluation on the Edge Device

After CNN had been trained used Keras framework with TensorFlow backend, it had been deployed to Kendryte K210 system-on-chip. Obtained CNN requires 23 660 bytes to store its structure and weights as well as 81 920 bytes to store intermediate features maps and other runtime data during the forward pass. Consequently, the method is lightweight enough to run on the edge device like Kendryte K210.

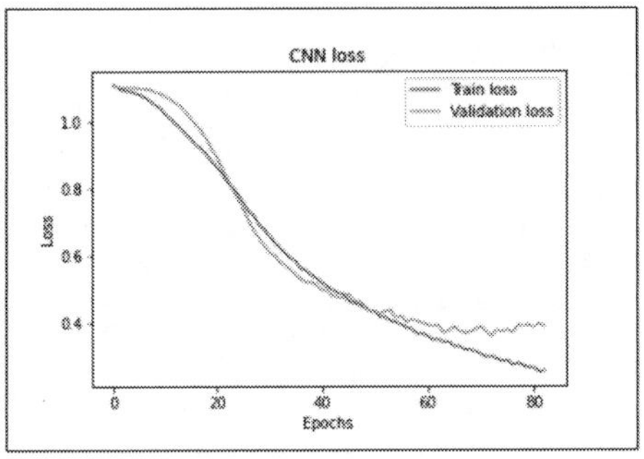

Figure 3. Training and validation loss curves of CNN.

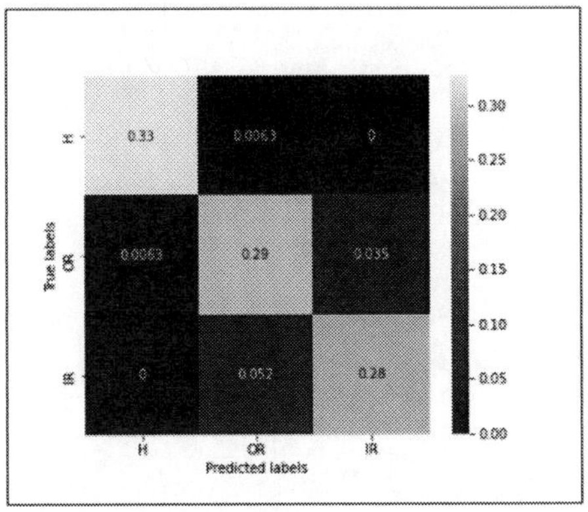

Figure 4. Confusion matrix of CNN on training data normalized over all population.

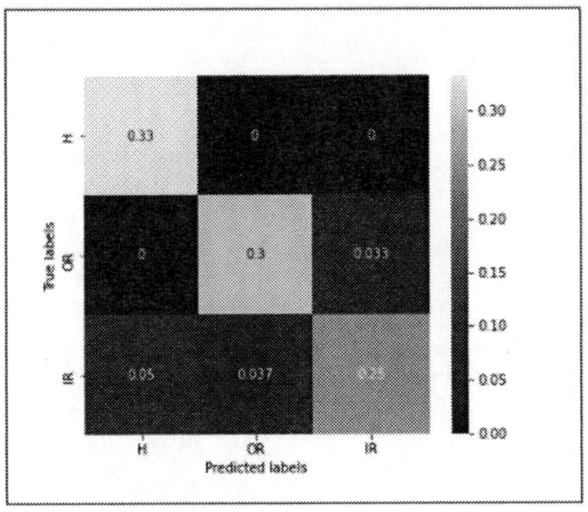

Figure 5. Confusion matrix of CNN on validation data normalized over all population.

The measured neural network execution time was 212 ms, which is approximately 1.66 times larger than the used frame size of the signal. Since in real applications, depending on the monitoring object, it is sufficient to carry out diagnostics once every $1 \ldots 10$ seconds, the purposed system could be able to monitor up to 50 units in real-time. In case the units are different and different CNN have to be used, it is possible to store in SRAM more than one CNN and use them in turn.

Depending on memory consumption by other applications, more than 200 CNNs like the one used in this paper could store simultaneously in SRAM. However, in this case, additional time would be spent on resources initialization and releasing. In our experiments, the initialization time of CNN and resources releasing time are about 3 ms and 90 us, respectively, which are significantly less than the CNN execution time.

The detailed analysis of the computation graph of CNN ported to Kendryte K210 revealed that only matrix multiplication in the first fully-connected layer is accelerated by the CNN hardware accelerator. This acceleration is possible by replacing of matrix multiplication by multiple convolutions, which is performed by neural network compiler nncase. The replacing consist in the conversion of matrix product of the weight matrix of shape (N, K) by the activation matrix of shape $(K, 1)$ to convolutional layer, whose number of filters is equal N and input is activation matrix of shape $(K, 1, 1)$, where the first dimension is channel number.

However, convolutional layers are processed by CPU without hardware acceleration, while those layers include most of the calculations. This is because CNN accelerator unit is only able to perform 1×1 or 3×3 convolution, while convolutional layers of our CNN have 1×64, 1×32, and 1×16 kernels, and there is no an algorithm in nncase utility to transform arbitrary convolution into a set of 1×1 or 3×3 convolutions. Hence, to further improve the performance, we need to develop CNN consist only of 1×1 or 3×3 convolutions or develop a method of transformation of arbitrary convolution into a set of 1×1 or 3×3 convolutions.

VI. CONCLUSION

This paper discussed the edge computing opportunities for fault diagnostics in industrial rotary machinery using CNN methods. We showed that the edge IoT device capacity is enough to make data analysis based on CNN. The analysis can be implemented in real-time, so online data analytics services can be provided to personnel near or remote the industrial production system.

ACKNOWLEDGMENT

This research is implemented in Petrozavodsk State University (PetrSU) with financial support by the Ministry of Science and Higher Education of Russia within Agreement no. 075-11-2019-088 of 20.12.2019 on the topic "Creating the high-tech production of mobile microprocessor computing modules based on SiP and PoP technology for smart data collection, mining, and interaction with surrounding sources".

REFERENCES

[1] D. Hasselquist, A. Rawat, and A. Gurtov, "Trends and detection avoidance of internet-connected industrial control systems," IEEE Access, vol. 7, 2019, pp. 155 504–155 512.

[2] K. Zhong, M. Han, and B. Han, "Data-driven based fault prognosis for industrial systems: a concise overview," IEEE/CAA Journal of Automatica Sinica, vol. 7, no. 2, 2020, pp. 330–345.

[3] C. Lessmeier, J. K. Kimotho, D. Zimmer, and W. Sextro, "Condition monitoring of bearing damage in electromechanical drive systems by using motor current signals of electric motors: A benchmark data set for data-driven classification," in Proceedings of the European conference of the prognostics and health management society, 2016, pp. 05–08.

[4] T. A. Shifat and J. W. Hur, "An effective stator fault diagnosis framework of bldc motor based on vibration and current signals," IEEE Access, vol. 8, 2020, pp. 106 968–106 981.

[5] S. Naveen and M. R. Kounte, "Key technologies and challenges in iot edge computing," in 2019 Third International conference on I-SMAC (IoT in Social, Mobile, Analytics and Cloud) (I-SMAC), 2019, pp. 61–65.

[6] L. Jing, T. Wang, M. Zhao, and P. Wang, "An adaptive multi-sensor data fusion method based on deep convolutional neural networks for fault diagnosis of planetary gearbox," Sensors, vol. 17, 02 2017, pp. 1–15.

[7] J.-R. Jiang, J.-E. Lee, and Y.-M. Zeng, "Time series multiple channel convolutional neural network with attention-based long short-term memory for predicting bearing remaining useful life," Sensors, vol. 20, no. 1, 2020, pp. 1–19.

[8] J. K. Kimotho and W. Sextro, "An approach for feature extraction and selection from non-trending data for machinery prognosis," in Proceedings of the second european conference of the prognostics and health management society, vol. 5, no. 4, 2014, pp. 1–8.

[9] D. Palossi et al., "A 64-mw dnn-based visual navigation engine for autonomous nano-drones," IEEE Internet of Things Journal, vol. 6, no. 5, 2019, pp. 8357–8371.

[10] D. Park, S. Kim, Y. An, and J. Y. Jung, "Lired: A light weight real time fault detection system for edge computing using lstm recurrent neural networks," Sensors, vol. 18, no. 7, 2018, p. 2110.

[11] "K210 Datasheet," 2019, URL: https://s3.cn-north-1.amazonaws.com.cn/dl.kendryte.com/documents/kendryte_datasheet_20181011163248_en.pdf [accessed: 2020-08-26].

[12] D. P. Kingma and J. Ba, "Adam: A method for stochastic optimization," arXiv preprint arXiv:1412.6980, 2014, pp. 1–15.

[13] "TensorFlow Lite converter," 2020, URL: https://www.tensorflow.org/lite/convert [accessed: 2020-08-26].

[14] "GitHub - kendryte/nncase: Open deep learning compiler stack for Kendryte K210 AI accelerator," 2020, URL: https://github.com/kendryte/nncase [accessed: 2020-08-26].

Robotic and Smart Service for People with Disabilities

Sergey Zavyalov
Petrozavodsk State University
Petrozavodsk, Russia
Email: sza123@list.ru

Anton Kogochev
Petrozavodsk State University
Petrozavodsk, Russia
Email: antkg@yandex.ru

Lyudmila Shchegoleva
Petrozavodsk State University
Petrozavodsk, Russia
Email: schegoleva@petrsu.ru

Abstract—**The article presents and discusses the problem of developing a robotic system for the care and supervision of people with disabilities. The main functions of the robotic system are telecommunications between patients and their guardians, automatic management of platform movement, manipulator movement and gripper. An overview of existing solutions (devices) on the robotics market that implement similar capabilities is presented. Each device is a complex and expensive system. In order for a robotic system to be widely accessible to all people, it is necessary to reduce the cost of its components. Inexpensive mechanical components have disadvantages in terms of movement accuracy. We propose a hypothesis about the possibility of using artificial intelligence to improve the accuracy of actions performed by a robotic system. Analysis of the video image of the manipulator movement can allow to adjust the speed and angle of rotation of the motors in the joints of the manipulator, thereby making the movements more accurate.**

Keywords–Robotics; Remote control; Manipulator; Alarm system; Smart capture.

I. INTRODUCTION

The value of human health and life is a priority for everyone individually and for humanity as a whole. The development of technologies allows to gradually exclude people from those processes where they are forced to work physically, monotonously and with a strain of attention. A special role in this process belongs to robotics.

Science fiction writers have formed the image of a robot as a thinking human-like mechanism that can interact with humans and the environment. In reality, robots are complex software and hardware complexes, mostly located in dark, unheated workshops, away from humans. The reason for the discrepancy between reality and ideas is the fact that human likeness or anthropomorphism is an extremely complex property. It is extremely difficult to create an artificial intelligence equal in flexibility and power to the human one. However, the ideal robot image remains as one of the goals of technology development, including mechatronics, sensors, electronics, mathematics, and information technology.

The level of technology development today allows us to replace a person with software and hardware systems that can perform part of human duties related to industrial production and other areas of activity.

Robots from workshops and fenced spaces step into the space of a human and the human is in the zone of action of robots. It is clear that such interaction should be effective and safe. Robots need to be adapted to human environment and to interact with people just like any of us.

A current trend in robotics is the development of robots for the social sphere of life of an individual and society as a whole [1].

If a robot becomes a part of a humans life, if it interacts with a person and has the intelligence to perform certain tasks, then it can be considered as part of the Ambient Intelligence [2].

The purpose of this research is to develop a robotic system designed for monitoring and telecommunications with people with disabilities, as well as to help them perform manipulations with various objects (for example, to pick up a fallen object). At the same time, the robotic system should not be bulky to move freely inside a small, limited room, and expensive to be accessible to patients with a low income level.

Nowadays, a robot for individuals is a complex and very expensive system. Low-cost components have a number of shortcomings, the main ones being non stability and non precision of movements. The main hypothesis is to use capabilities of artificial intelligence to compensate shortcomings of low-cost components and to construct robotics system available for any person.

The rest of this paper is organized as follows. Section II describes the robotic system proposed, its designated purpose, main functions and architecture. Section III lists the main problems that arise when implementing a robotic system and required solutions using artificial intelligence. Each of the listed tasks can be considered as a separate one, without reference to the robotic system proposed. There are various approaches to solve these tasks. The most relevant approaches are presented in Section IV. Some of the approaches have already been implemented to some extent in existing robots. Section V describes the existing robotic systems, in which some tasks are partially solved. We conclude the work in Section VI.

II. DESCRIPTION OF THE ROBOTIC SYSTEM

Robotics technology can be deployed in healthcare [3]. Robotics for healthcare presents a major research challenge due to the strong requirements to deal with humans. The proposed solution belongs to the assistive robotics subdomain. This subdomain requires more flexible and compact systems able to navigate in public areas, to grasp and manipulate soft and delicate objects as stated in the Multi-Annual Roadmap For Robotics in Europe [1]. Great importance is attached to the use of artificial intelligence in such systems.

The aim of this research is to develop a robotic system designed for the care and supervision of people with disabilities (patients). There are often cases when the patient lives alone, or remains alone for a long time. At the same time, the patient can have certain autonomy, but can not be left unattended. It is also important for the patient to communicate, first of all with their guardian (relatives) and to have the psychological confidence that they will not be abandoned and can ask for help at any time. In such a situation, the best decision, of course, is to have some person that will be constantly near the patient. A human person can look after a patient, serve him, help him, and talk to him. But, at the same time, a human person can get tired and distracted. In addition, the number of such people should be quite large.

The robotic system being developed is designed to replace a person in such a situation.

The system functions include remote manual and autonomous movement in an indoor environment (house, apartment, ward), two-way video data exchange in real time between the patient and their guardian, tracking the patient's condition, detecting dangerous conditions of the patient and transmitting an alarm signal to the guardian or immediately to the rescue service, remote manual and autonomous control of the manipulator and the gripper.

To implement these functions, the robotic system must have a wheeled platform, a manipulator with a gripper, a video camera, a screen, a set of sensors, a wireless data transmission system, and a system controller. The robot is controlled in autonomous mode and in manual or semi-autonomous mode with the remote device.

This architecture has a number of advantages. Through the use of the manipulator, there is an opportunity to interact with objects located near the robot. For example, give the patient a bottle of water or pick up a fallen item from the floor. The video camera and screen provide a two-way exchange of video data in real time using the Internet, as well as allow the robot to receive commands from the patient, and allow the operator to remotely manage the platform and the manipulator. The system controller provides interaction of all subsystems of the robot. The set of sensors includes sensors for determining the distance to objects, for measuring the force effect. Sensors can also include a video camera and microphone.

Thus, the patient and their guardian can be separated in space at any distance within a sufficiently high-speed Internet, staying constantly in touch. The guardian is able to remotely provide assistance within the capabilities of the manipulator.

A prototype of the robotic system will be presented at the St. Petersburg Technical Fair (PTFair) 2020.

III. Tasks of the Robotic System

The robotic system must operate in manual mode and automatic mode. Its main actions are the movement of the platform, movement of the manipulator and clamping the gripper. When performing these actions in manual mode, the operator (guardian) controls all mechanisms (wheel motors, manipulator servos and gripper), relying on the video image transmitted from a video camera installed on the platform, as well as from video cameras permanently installed in the room. Even under these conditions, the completeness of the view may not be achieved, and the accuracy and safety of the movements may not be sufficient to achieve the goal. Therefore, in manual control mode, the system needs help to ensure that these criteria are met. Moreover, these criteria become more relevant, when robotic system work in automatic mode.

Let us formulate the important tasks for managing the robotic platform that require solutions in the field of artificial intelligence:

- Creation of the route of the platform movement, avoiding dynamically appearing obstacles, recognizing their shape and gaining experience in circumventing them, and possibly moving them to free the passage;
- Creation of the trajectory of the manipulator with similar functions, but different degrees of freedom;
- Selection of the position to capture depending on the shape of the object to be manipulated;
- The choice of the grabbing force depends on the characteristics of the object to be manipulated, so that on the one hand the object will not be broken, and on the other hand the object will not fall (is firmly held);
- The prediction actions in repetitive situations of working with objects and obstacles;
- The detection abnormalities in the patient's behaviour and deciding whether to trigger an alarm.

Navigation, perception and cognition technologies provide a robot with the means to measure and interpret its environment, to learn of intelligent behaviour. During care processes, the database of typical motion and interaction patterns can be accumulated by the robots themselves and transferred to a shared knowledge base. Then, this knowledge will be used as needed from this shared repository, thus this will be a novel network ecosystem for robots.

A network centralized knowledge base and remote data processing will reduce the energy requirements for individual computing nodes of robotic systems. These nodes themselves can be simpler and cheaper. In addition, the released resources could be spent on improving the ergonomics of the design of the robotic system.

Thus, it is the task of computer vision with deep processing of the scene and environment surveillance, the task of the obtaining additional information about objects from the Internet and the task of the gaining experience in manipulating with various objects. That is the core of the intelligent system.

IV. Overview of Solutions Being Developed

The problem of path planning for an automation moving in a two-dimensional space has been known for a long time [4]. Navigation in indoor environment can occur in conditions where the map or plan of the place is known and when such a map needs to be made first. When generating a route, it is necessary to take into account the dimensions of the robotic platform, as well as possible angles of its rotation. In the course of patient activity, the location of objects may change, which leads to generation of new routes in real time [5]. Now, the ways to get information about the surrounding space are being improved, the ability to process large amounts of information is being accelerated, and path planning algorithms based on the use of various types of information and deep processing of information are being developed [6].

The sources of information are lidars that measure distances to surrounding objects in the range of 360 degrees, video cameras, stereo-video cameras that receive flat and three-dimensional images in different electromagnetic wave spectra.

The movement is transferred from a flat surface to a surface that has a slope, where the power of the motors needs to be taken into account to overcome the path. The movement is considered in three-dimensional space and the path is being created for flying robots that must avoid obstacles from left, right, above and below.

Truly smart devices must correctly identify obstacles. If glasses are lying on the floor, the smart mobile robot must understand that this is not just an uneven surface, but an extra object lying on the floor. Is it possible to drive through it? Should the robot go around the object? No, the glasses must be picked up and put in a safe place. These tasks have not yet been solved. For example, systems like Smart Walkers implement some of these functions and are designed to help people who have problems related to balance and gait stability [7].

Determining the trajectory of movement is also necessary for the manipulator. This task is even more difficult, since the manipulator has a greater number of degrees of freedom and operates in more complex conditions of external space. Its task is not only to achieve the goal, but also not to hook other objects with the manipulator. In [8], a vision system is used to recognize both different target objects and their poses that allow the robot to do pick-and-place operation, that includes selecting the gripper type or the grip angle.

The theoretical base of the planning and implementation of fast and absolute path accuracy motions for industrial manipulators constrained to a given geometric path is developed in [9][10]. The asymptotic orbital stabilization of motions and a novel analytical method for analysis and redesign of system's dynamics is achieved by use of a feedback control.

The next problem is gentle grabbing. One of the solutions is based on an electrically controllable adhesion mechanism [11]. In [12], a mobile robot able to autonomously pick-up from the floor objects a human is pointing at is presented. The robot decides by itself if an object is suitable for grasping by considering measures of size, position and the environment suitability.

V. OVERVIEW OF EXISTING DEVICES

Today, robotization takes place most actively in the following civil industries:

- Transport and logistics
- Agriculture, forestry, water management
- Medicine
- Production
- Civil infrastructure
- Commerce and service

A. *Transport and logistics*

In this industry, there are three close areas:

- Unmanned vehicles (cargo and passenger)
- Remote inspection systems for complex or dangerous objects
- Warehouse automated systems

A lot of publications are devoted to the progress of driverless vehicles. This direction is the most promising and closest to the production of final products.

To solve the problem of remote inspection of complex objects, autonomous systems are used. They operate in automatic and semi-automatic mode. A special feature of these systems is the need to operate at a great distance from the operator, in conditions where direct control is not possible. In such situations, autonomous systems are forced to solve the problem of moving along a given trajectory along the object under study in offline mode, relying on a system of sensors and artificial intelligence. In the case of flying and floating systems, it is necessary to take into account and compensate for the unpredictable effects of wind or water currents.

Flyability Elios (Figure 1) is the world's first flying robot for technical inspection of industrial facilities and search and rescue operations. It implements the following functions: search for injured climbers in the cracks of the glacier; visual and thermal inspection of steam boilers; inspection of container ship's ballast tanks; inspection and monitoring of mining equipment [13].

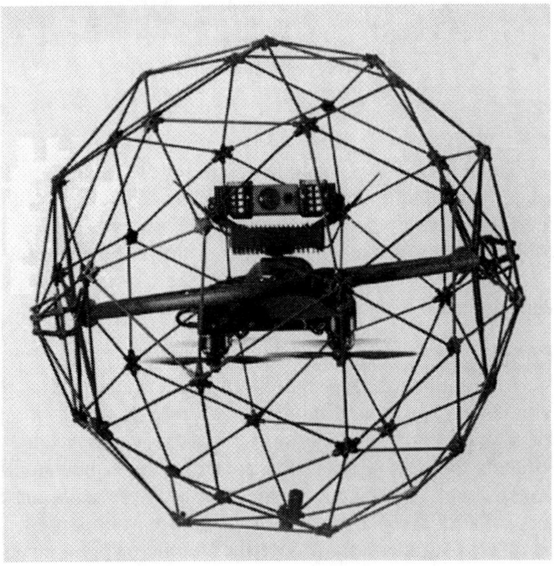

Figure 1. Flying robot Flyability Elios [14].

The Naturaldrones StillFly flying robot is designed to survey high voltage power lines using multispectral and high resolution cameras [15]. It operates under the operator's control in semi-automatic mode. It allows to monitor the condition of wires and structures of high-voltage supports.

The warehouse robots that transport goods in Amazon warehouses are 4-5 times more efficient than the company's employees who perform similar work [16].

B. *Agriculture and forestry management*

There is no doubt that there are many heavy, monotonous, strenuous activities in this industry that humans would be happy to hand over to robots.

The ecoRobotix weeding robot is equipped with a computer vision system designed to identify weeds. After detecting a weed, the robot sprays it with a small dose of herbicide [17].

AGROBOT E-Series (Figure 2) is the first robotic harvester for careful strawberry harvesting [18]. The flexible platform is equipped with 24 independent manipulators, easily adapts to any farm configuration, and is able to work at night. The robot is able to determine the location of the berry and its level of ripeness in real time. To solve this problem, graphics processors are used that process information received from short-range integrated color and infrared depth sensors. Manipulators are able to grab the stalk of a ripe berry selected by the AI with high precision, then cut the stalk and move the fruit into a special transport container without harming the berry. The developers also took care of the safety of people interacting with the robot. Special lidars take care of the safety of the surrounding field workers. Crossing the virtual perimeter stops the work of the robot, so as not to harm the person.

Figure 2. AGROBOT E-Series [18].

TreeRover is a Canadian robot for the planting of trees when conducting regeneration works [19]. A cassette with seedlings and a special burrowing device is installed on the robot's wheel platform. The robot follows the route based on GPS data and places seedlings from the cassette at a specified distance from each other along the way.

C. Medicine

A prominent representative of clinical systems is the Da Vinci robot surgeon (Figure 3), designed for performing surgical operations [20]. As an executive device, it allows the surgeon to see the operation area in a high-precision three-dimensional format and operate with high-precision manipulators in hard-to-reach places. In the future, robot surgeons will be able to significantly reduce the trauma of operations, making them remotely through small incisions. It is also possible that the movements of the scalpel and other instruments will be synchronized with the breathing, heartbeat and other micro-movements of patients, which will also increase the safety of operations and reduce the number of tissue injuries.

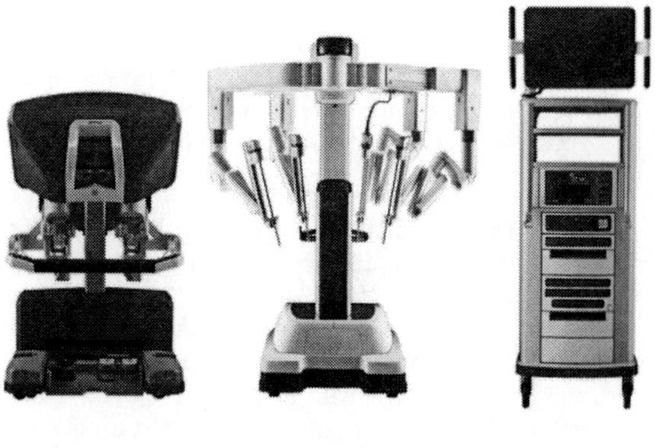

Figure 3. The da Vinci surgical system [21].

Auxiliary medical robots perform the functions of nannies and nurses. Robear (Figure 4) is the most developed representative of this group of robots. The robot presented in [22] is the third experimental example of a robot that can lift a patient out of bed and put him in a wheelchair. It is equipped with sensors that allow it to avoid colliding with medical staff, patients, furniture and fit into doorways. A particularly important quality of auxiliary medical robots is human safety. A patient can be moved only in a narrow range of accelerations, be touched only with carefully dosed effort and in precisely defined places.

Figure 4. Experimental nursing care robot Robear [23].

D. Cobots for production

Apart from specialized robots, it should be consider such types of robots as cobots (collaborative robots) (for example, cobots Hanwha2 (Figure 5)). Their purpose is to perform work in the same workspace with a person, without causing harm to them [24]. Collaborative robots are used in small companies where it is necessary to quickly and frequently reconfigure production lines and integrate them into the existing production process. Cobots successfully cope with complex, monotonous physical actions, without requiring a salary increase and a lunch break. But the main advantage of such robots is their safety for humans when performing joint actions. In addition, collaborative robots are open systems, which allows us to program them to perform exactly the actions that are required at the moment, as well as reprogram them after to perform other actions.

E. Applicability of the solutions presented

Among the developments listed above, the most suitable for implemented the functions we are interested in is AGROBOT. It includes "Real Time Artificial Intelligence" for determining ripe berry of strawberry, but, only strawberry. It provides human safety, but it moves only in a special organized space. It provides precise moving to target and gentle grabbing. Table I presents the main features of the robotic systems listed.

Thus, the market already has solutions that allow to implement almost all the functionality of the proposed robotic system. At the same time, the cost of such a solution will be quite high. On the other hand, low-cost components allow to

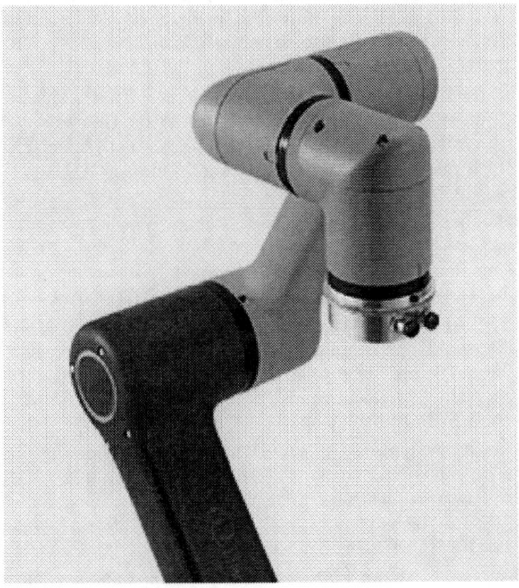

Figure 5. Cobot Hanwha HCR-5 [25].

TABLE I. FEATURES OF ROBOTIC SYSTEMS

Robotic systems	*Features*
Flyability Elios	• Obstacle avoidance • Eliminating potential harm to workers • Video translation
Naturaldrones StillFly	• Obstacle avoidance • Video translation
Amazon warehouse robots	• Route planning • Obstacle avoidance
ecoRobotix	• Computer vision • Object recognition • The targeting an object
AGROBOT E-Series	• Computer vision • Object recognition • The targeting an object • Gentle grabbing • Human security
TreeRover	• Route planning • Manipulation
Da Vinci	• Exceptional accuracy • Manipulation • Video translation
Robear	• Route planning • Obstacle avoidance • Manipulation • Gentle grabbing
Hanhwa	• Manipulation • Human security

get a similar product, but with rather poor characteristics of movement accuracy. And here, too, artificial intelligence can come to help. The capabilities of artificial intelligence with use of feedback control can compensate for the shortcomings of the mechanical system.

One of the main problems in the development of the system is mechanical flaws in the design of the manipulator and the servos used in it, which do not guarantee an accurate rotation at a given angle. Each movement is performed with a small error, which accumulates in several joints of the manipulator, leading to a significant error in reaching the target position. It is of interest to investigate the trajectories of the manipulator using tracking with a video camera and teach the manipulator to adjust the speed and angle of rotation of the motors in its joints by analysing the video image. This approach is based on methods presented in [10]. Memorizing the movements will allow to use them in subsequent operations. An important point here is the establishment of the limits of the motor errors, within which compensation is still possible, since in other cases compensation can lead to oscillations around the target without reaching it.

Artificial intelligence will be used to analyze video images and other sensors data and to form a knowledge base for manipulating manipulator elements in similar external conditions.

The functionality of the system being developed is supposed to be endowed with the system properties listed below.

Configurability – the ability to easily and quickly reconfigure software and hardware to maximize the system's compliance with a wide range of tasks.

Adaptability – a response to changes in the work environment, including the ability to self-learn and apply autoconfiguration strategies.

Interaction – the ability to interact with the operator, patients, other robots, and other systems in the work environment.

Mobility – the ability to move in relation to the kinematics and dynamics of manipulators, as well as positioning and navigation within the working environment.

Manipulation – the ability to handle material objects and tools, regardless of their shape, density and trajectory of movement, approximately as a person does in natural conditions.

Perception - the ability to choose the measurement method, to perform an effective analysis of signals and data received from a complex of heterogeneous sensors, as well as to obtain the maximum information output from the available data.

Autonomy – the ability to determine of the maximum level of responsibility in the processes of system management, task control, taking into account the context when interacting with the patient, the operator and the work environment.

Cognition – the ability to implement functions that reduce programming and configuration requirements in deployed systems.

The implementation of these system features will allow to create a system that fully corresponds to the task at hand, while being safe for humans, easy to intuitively manage and quite flexible in both hardware and software.

VI. CONCLUSION

This article examines the problem of developing a robotic system for the elderly and people with disabilities. The main purpose of the system is related to the implementation of the telecommunications of the patient with the guardian, of the remote manual control of platform and manipulator by the guardian, and the autonomous control of the platform and the manipulator. The implementation of a robotic device requires solving a number of theoretical and technical problems. For this purpose, the review of the current state of industrial robotics and analytical problems of control was performed. As a result, it was shown that the theoretical problems of constructing the route of the platform, manipulator and gripper are partially solved. The considered robotic systems used in various sectors of the economy have the functions and characteristics that the developed system should have. At the same time, there is no device that fully meets the stated requirements on the market yet. The implementation of some functions, in particular, the correct capture of objects that differ in structure and properties, is not represented in existing robotic devices. In addition, all implemented devices have a high cost, which makes it difficult to use them widely. In addition, the problem of population ageing is becoming more urgent. The article hypothesizes that expensive components can be replaced with cheaper, but less accurate ones. To overcome the emerging problem of movement accuracy and solve the problem of universal capture, it is proposed to use artificial intelligence. In the future, it is planned to conduct experiments to test the hypothesis and determine the limits of applicability of artificial intelligence methods for correcting inaccurate manipulator movements. This will allow to create robotic systems that are more adapted to the diversity of the real world and more versatile and flexible.

In general, it is shown that robotic systems are actively implemented in the professional activity and daily life of a person. Solving the problem of reducing the cost of robotic systems will lead to a wider introduction of robotics into everyday life, which will make human life longer and more comfortable.

ACKNOWLEDGMENT

This research is implemented in Petrozavodsk State University (PetrSU) with financial support by the Ministry of Science and Higher Education of Russia within Agreement no. 075-11-2019-088 of 20.12.2019 on the topic "Creating the high-tech production of mobile microprocessor computing modules based on SiP and PoP technology for smart data collection, mining, and interaction with surrounding sources". The work is performed within the Government Program of Flagship University Development for Petrozavodsk State University (PetrSU) in 2017–2021.

REFERENCES

[1] "Robotics 2020 Multi-Annual Roadmap For Robotics in Europe," Horizon 2020 Call ICT-2017 (ICT-25, ICT-27 and ICT-28), 2016.

[2] D. Korzun, E. Balandina, A. Kashevnik, S.Balandin, and F. Viola, "Ambient Intelligence Services in IoT Environments: Emerging Research and Opportunities," IGI Global, 2019, ISBN13: 9781522589730. http://doi:10.4018/978-1-5225-8973-0

[3] S. Kar, "Robotics in HealthCare," in 2nd International Conference on Power Energy, Environment and Intelligent Control (PEEIC), Greater Noida, India, 2019, pp. 78-83, doi: https://doi.org/10.1109/PEEIC47157.2019.8976668.

[4] S. M. LaValle, "Planning Algorithms," Cambridge University Press, May 29, 2006.

[5] H. J. S. Feder and J-J. E. Slotine, "Real-time path planning using harmonic potentials in dynamic environments," in Proceedings of IEEE International Conference on Robotics and Automation, Albuquerque, NM, April 1997, pp. 874-881.

[6] K. A. Muteb, "Vision-Based Mobile Robot Map Building and Environment Fuzzy Learning," 2014 5th International Conference on Intelligent Systems, Modelling and Simulation, Langkawi, 2014, pp. 43-48, doi: 10.1109/ISMS.2014.155.

[7] S. D. Sierra, J. F. Molina, D. A. Gómez, M. C. Múnera, and C. A. Cifuentes, "Development of an Interface for Human-Robot Interaction on a Robotic Platform for Gait Assistance: AGoRA Smart Walker," 2018 IEEE ANDESCON, Santiago de Cali, 2018, pp. 1-7, doi: 10.1109/ANDESCON.2018.8564594.

[8] H. Lin, Y. Chen, and Y. Chen, "Robot vision to recognize both object and rotation for robot pick-and-place operation," 2015 International Conference on Advanced Robotics and Intelligent Systems (ARIS), Taipei, 2015, pp. 1-6, doi: 10.1109/ARIS.2015.7158364

[9] S. S. Pchelkin, A. S. Shiriaev, A. Robertsson, and L. B. Freidovich, "Integrated time-optimal trajectory planning and control design for industrial robot manipulator," 2013 IEEE/RSJ International Conference on Intelligent Robots and Systems, Tokyo, 2013, pp. 2521-2526, doi: 10.1109/IROS.2013.6696711

[10] S. S. Pchelkin et al., "On Orbital Stabilization for Industrial Manipulators: Case Study in Evaluating Performances of Modified PD+ and Inverse Dynamics Controllers," in IEEE Transactions on Control Systems Technology, vol. 25, no. 1, pp. 101-117, Jan. 2017, doi: 10.1109/TCST.2016.2554520

[11] J. Guo, J. Leng, and J. Rossiter, "Electroadhesion Technologies for Robotics: A Comprehensive Review," in IEEE Transactions on Robotics, vol. 36, no. 2, pp. 313-327, April 2020, doi: 10.1109/TRO.2019.2956869.

[12] P. De La Puente, D. Fischinger, M. Bajones, D. Wolf, and M. Vincze, "Grasping Objects From the Floor in Assistive Robotics: Real World Implications and Lessons Learned," in IEEE Access, vol. 7, pp. 123725-123735, 2019, doi: 10.1109/ACCESS.2019.2938366.

[13] "Raw Video: Drone Used to Inspect Huge Boiler", URL: https://www.youtube.com/watch?v=_nMdSb0X5bo&feature=youtu.be [retrieved: July, 2020]

[14] "FLYABILITY", URL: https://www.flyability.com/elios/ [retrieved: July, 2020]

[15] "Drone (ND StillFly) for Power Lines Monitoring", URL: https://www.youtube.com/watch?v=xsMqk2BPheQ [retrieved: July, 2020]

[16] "Roboty-kladovshchiki Amazon rabotayut v 5 raz effektivnee lyudei", URL: https://www.youtube.com/watch?v=nQty01yjV9I [retrieved: July, 2020]

[17] "ecoRobotix", URL: http://robotrends.ru/robopedia/ecorobotix/ [retrieved: July, 2020]

[18] "AGROBOT", URL: https://www.agrobot.com/e-series/ [retrieved: July, 2020]

[19] "TreeRover – robot dlya vysadki derev'ev", URL: http://robocraft.ru/blog/news/3419.html [retrieved: July, 2020]

[20] "Demonstratsiya raboty robota-khirurga davinchi", URL: https://www.youtube.com/watch?v=JT1b3QHi64o [retrieved: July, 2020]

[21] "About da Vinci Systems", URL: https://www.davincisurgery.com/da-vinci-systems/about-da-vinci-systems [retrieved: July, 2020]

[22] "Samyi milyi robot truditsya v meditsine", URL: https://www.youtube.com/watch?v=N3kgxardbqA [retrieved: July, 2020]

[23] "The strong robot with the gentle touch", URL: https://www.riken.jp/en/news_pubs/research_news/pr/2015/20150223_2/ [retrieved: July, 2020]

[24] "Koboty Hanwha: obzor lineiki kollaborativnykh robotov Hanwha HCR-3, HCR-5, HCR-12", URL: https://www.youtube.com/watch?v=J30bkx5f9aU [retrieved: July, 2020]

[25] "A variety of HCR robots to meet your needs", URL: https://www.hanwharobotics.com/ [retrieved: July, 2020]

Edge-Centric Video Data Analytics for Smart Assistance Services in Industrial Systems

Nikita A. Bazhenov, Artur E. Harkovchuk, Dmitry G. Korzun

Department of Computer Science
Petrozavodsk State University (PetrSU)
Petrozavodsk, Russia
e-mail: {bazhenov, harkovch, dkorzun}@cs.petrsu.ru

Abstract—**Video data analytics has now become essentially oriented on edge-centric computing in Internet of Things (IoT). In this paper, we consider such video services that provide analytics to smart assistance in industrial IoT systems. We identify the opportunities of industrial video data analytics. We present an edge-centric architecture for constructing smart assistance services. Based on this architecture, we implemented several pilot services that demonstrate the opportunities of industrial video data analytics. The services are deployed and experimented in a real enterprise for monitoring industrial production equipment (technical state and its evolution, ongoing production processes, equipment operating conditions).**

Keywords–Video data analytics; Internet of Things; Smart Assistance Services; Edge-Centric Computing.

I. Introduction

Internet of Things (IoT) supports the development of smart environments, where the key element is a smart service [1]. The service intelligence is essentially based on data analytics. In the case of video data, a smart service provides video surveillance and visual interactivity with the user [2]. Such a service provides analytical information about the object under monitoring [3].

Video data analytics has now become essentially oriented on edge-centric computing in the Internet of Things (IoT) [4], [5]. In this paper, we consider services that provide video data analytics to smart assistance in industrial IoT systems. Our Industrial Partner to deploy and experiment with the services is Petrozavodskmash, which is a branch of AEM-technology JSC in the Petrozavodsk city (Republic of Karelia, Russia). The company is one of the largest machine-building enterprises based on the following industries: foundry, welding, and mechanical assembly production.

The challanging problem is performing video data processing on edge devices, which are of low capacity and computing power [1]. In this paper, we show that a solution to this problem moves industrial video data analytics to the next level with respect to the "real-time assistance" property of the smart services. We consider an edge-centric architecture for constructing such smart assistance services in Industrial IoT (IIoT) systems.

Based on this architecture, we implemented several pilot services to demonstrate the opportunities for industrial video data analytics.

- Monitoring mechanical components of equipment to detect deviations in machine operations;
- Operator presence in the area to control production processes;
- Screen image text analysis from the Computer Numerical Control (CNC) display monitor to detect errors.

The services are deployed and experimented for monitoring industrial production equipment (technical state and its evolution, ongoing production processes, equipment operating conditions).

The rest of the paper is organized as follows. Section II considers existing methods and example services in edge-centric video data analytics. Section III identifies the opportunities of video data analytics based on the needs of our Industrial Partner. Section IV presents our edge-centric architecture for constructing smart assistance services. Finally, Section V concludes the paper.

II. Related work

The current focus on edge-centric in IoT systems supports high efficiency and throughput of the processed information [6], as well as provides additional opportunities for connecting multiple devices. Edge-centric allows us to organize decentralized computing on multiple edge devices, using limited resources between participants in the space. Many systems use mobile devices at the edge [7], which allows for more efficient distribution between devices. The organization of such a computation model makes it possible to reduce the computation time of the most complex algorithms that require a large resource of time for preprocessing and analysis.

Many solutions integrate existing IoT concepts into more comprehensively organized structures. A particular example is the combination of several video surveillance devices into a common video system behind a complex object: the smart home. Smart homes are combined into smart cities [8], which makes it possible to control systems such as ecology, security, safety, and health of citizens on a global level. Modern monitoring systems are able to diagnose the working condition of machines in real-time. This allows for early detection of deviations and breakdowns that occur with equipment during active production [9]. As monitoring tools, sensors, or sensor networks is mainly used to measure various indicators of the current state of machines (e.g., current consumption, temperature, accelerometer values). Such sensors are installed in the internal system of the equipment or are connected separately from the equipment.

During the operation, machines generate vibrations which result in the deterioration of machine tools eventually causing failure of some subsystems or the machine itself [10]. The vibration signatures analysis can be used to detect the nature and extent of any damage in machines and components or any maintenance decisions related to the machine. However, modern industrial monitoring systems mainly use sensors to detect a large number of defects. Thus, the breakage verification criterion is based solely on sensor readings. The use of video services makes it possible to expand the empirical picture of the breakdown of machinery, even when a video camera is watching an object.

Thus, the closest solutions to the developed solution are the following scientific works: recognition of worker activity in a factory using convolutional neural networks [11], recognition of workers who are not wearing a safety helmet [12], error recognition based on text from CNC monitor [13].

III. Industrial Video Data Analytics

The Petrozavodskmash company is a machine-building enterprise with a huge database of machine tools working in various industries. We use our industrial partner to deploy and experiment with our pilot smart assistance services for monitoring industrial production equipment (technical state and its evolution, ongoing production processes, equipment operating conditions).

A. Methods

The key solution of the method is the use of edge computing, which includes well-known mathematical processing algorithms (for example, motion recognition on a video camera, image rendering, combining information video streams), semantic data mining (separation of relationships and relationships between streams) and performing calculations using several heterogeneous resources of video cameras and personal mobile devices available in the peripheral IoT environment on different mobile platforms.

Semantic integration will take place at the level of the IoT environment, using the available resources of the surrounding equipment to obtain data for observing objects. In particular, efficiency gains will be achieved through: connecting a large number of video cameras and processing on devices with low performance; the use of Artificial Intelligence (AI) technologies; calculating heterogeneous data analyzed on the basis of images from a video camera; using the Semantic Web and finding connections between video streams. Modern video data analysis systems for recognizing people, objects and zones, are described in [14].

The integration between smart video surveillance and IoT is described in [15]. The authors show how different objects, cameras, and sensors can process various pieces of information in the network. The authors propose an innovative topology paradigm that shows better communication between different video camera surveillance systems provided by IoT.

B. Multi-platform monitoring and computing

Multi-platform development of the mobile applications [16] refers to applications that can work both on mobile (Android, Apple) and desktop (PC, Windows) devices. One of the important advantages is the development of a distributed application that can run on several platforms at the same time, including adjusting to its interface depending on the mobile platform, screen resolution, orientation, and the user's own wishes. The main requirement is to create a combined desktop and Web application presented as a single development environment.

However, the most efficient implementation of multiplatform is to create a hybrid application [17] that runs on multiple platforms simultaneously. The simplest implementation method is to integrate applications into the user's Web browser that is used on each platform. Thus, the display of services will be implemented using their uniform representation for users in the form of an HTML page. All the user needs to do is have Internet access or a local router connection.

C. Edge analytics

An edge-centric parametric predictive analytics methodology is shown in [18]. The use of such a methodology uses predictive data analytics and ensures that only the information that is needed is transmitted. This point is especially important during analysis on the IoT edge, as video data is generally very large for processing and transmission, which creates a huge load on the server and network.

The main advantage is the extraction of the necessary video frames from the stream. Thus, processing incoming frames in real-time, although it will take up most of the processor time, will reduce the load on the network and the occupied space on the local data storage.

D. Heterogeneous data

Knowledge graphs can be used to implement edge analytics in some heterogeneous environments [4]. Since video analytics will be performed in real-time, various pieces of information will be received by users. Instead of the entire video stream, only keyframes that are meaningful to users will be used. Moreover, these frames will be preprocessed in advance and they will contain information that is important for solving a particular task (for example, determining the number of workers in the machine tool area). In addition, instead of frames, it can only be a text or graphic notification about the current state of the equipment. The most complete and advanced delivery option will be the use of graphs, charts, histograms with distribution over time.

Let us count the time between the incident and the operator's reaction. The system requires an average of 1 to 2 seconds to compute. Visible cases (defects) can be detected manually by a person within a few seconds or minutes. Invisible cases (which cannot be detected immediately) can be detected within hours or days. Manual viewing of all video recordings from cameras requires man-hours and also involves all the problems associated with the human factor.

The Video Event Representation Model is shown in Fig. 1. As an example, a service for recognizing people and calculating the distance to a person and equipment is used. The first video camera mounted on top of the machine area contains a video stream with people (machine operators) and also contains a video stream with the equipment. The second video camera is located at the level of human height and is necessary to recognize the helmets worn on the heads of operators (to comply with safety regulations). The third video camera is located at the level of the CNC monitor and is designed to recognize the error code that appears on the screen. Other IoT elements are also located next to the video cameras: an accelerometer, current clamp, temperature, tachometer (however, we will not discuss it at the level of the architecture). First, the connection to the database is initialized, from where the current information about the availability of

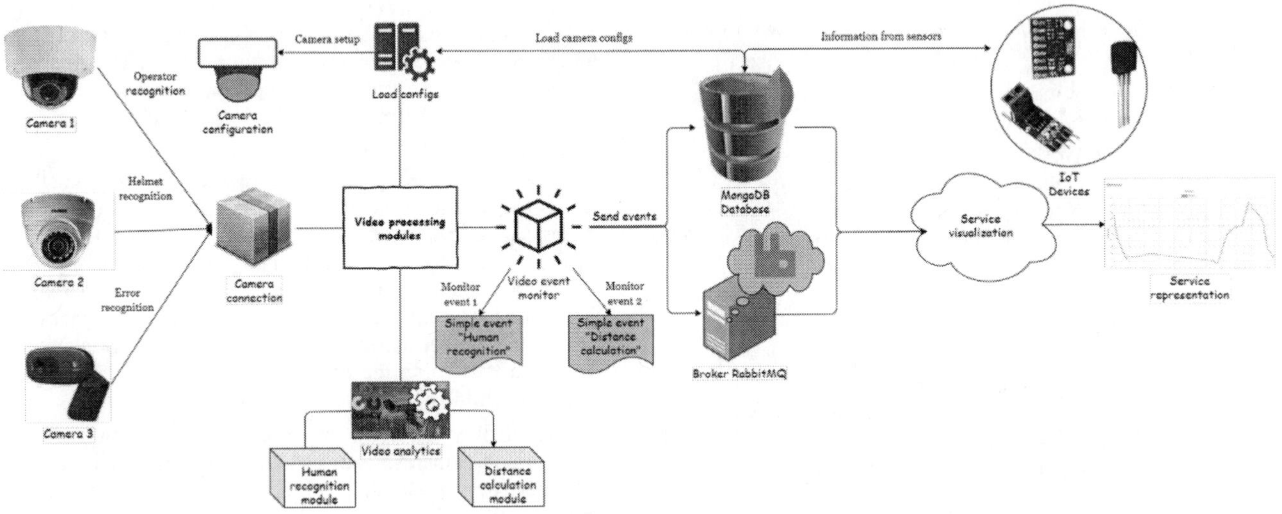

Figure 1. Video Event Representation Model

personnel in the area is taken, as well as the distance to the machinery. Cameras are connected to a router and transmit information to video processing modules. The video analytics modules (module for recognizing a person and calculating the distance) determine the presence of a person in the frame and also determine the distance to him by the silhouette of a person (it is assumed that the silhouette of a person in the frame is always fully visible). Further, events are generated using the monitor and sent to the MongoDB database, as well as to the RabbitMQ message broker. Further, the information is converted into the information necessary for users (building graphs and diagrams) and displayed in video services on the Web on end devices.

Each of the video cameras is used to provide the user with the specific information he needs. This allows the operator to receive real-time information about incidents involving people and machinery in the plant. Let us discuss the benefits of our solution. The applied architectural approach allows us to consider specific services from a practical point of view and deploy and use them in a specific enterprise. In particular, this approach is easy to understand and does not require a detailed explanation of the details. High performance is achieved through the use of automated recognition tools.

IV. Edge-Centric Video Data Analytics

The proposed architecture is based on the following properties:

- multiple video cameras to use, which provide various video data flows to be processed and analyzed;
- microservices to construct a dynamic system of services;
- edge-centric to implement an essential part of analytics locally (near the data sources).

In conditions of work in an unfavorable environment, a video surveillance camera protected from moisture and dust is used to obtain a video stream in real-time with its subsequent processing. The use of cameras that are not equipped with this protection requires the use of external protective boxes.

A. Monitoring mechanical components of equipment to detect deviations in machine operations

Consider the following objects for monitoring.

- Shock detection of moving parts of equipment [19].
- Detection of mounted rotary swivel head.
- Counterweight detection.

Monitoring the mechanical elements of the machine using video cameras allows us to automatically monitor the performance of the machine elements for the smooth operation of the machine. Elements that are attachments for the operation of the machine are tracked: counterweight and swivel head. For mounted elements, it is required to monitor: whether it is necessary to install, what is installed, whether it is installed correctly. External influences on the machine (impacts) are also monitored.

The use of the multi-platform allows the operator to control the correct operation of the machine, using a smartphone, without being at his work computer. The use of a smartphone allows us to increase efficiency and response to an event that has occurred since when an abnormality occurs, the operator processes all receive notifications in real-time.

Calculations are carried out on a central computer located near the machine. Computing near the machine helps to avoid the problem of transmitting large amounts of data over the network and to increase the processing speed.

The operator is provided with information about the rotary heads located on the storage rack, as well as the set angles of rotation of each of the heads. Depending on the head and the angle of rotation, a composite event is generated that notifies the operator whether the head is correctly or incorrectly positioned. The impacts of the moving parts of the machine are monitored and the information is transferred to the operator. The presence of the installed counterweight on the head is monitored. Depending on whether the counterweight is installed and the type of installed head, a composite event is generated about the requirement to install a counterweight to avoid incorrect operation of the machine.

B. Operator monitoring in the area to control production processes

1) Operator memorization and identification by his external characteristics:
   - Work uniform recognition;
   - Helmet recognition;
   - Human and face recognition;
   - Operator identification to gain access to the machine area.
2) Determination of the presence of the operator in the danger zone of the equipment:
   - Operator recognition [5];
   - Equipment recognition [20];
   - Detection of current distance to operator, to equipment;
   - Operator is in the danger zone of the equipment based on distances.

Tracking the presence of the operator on the site allows us to ensure the safety of the work process and control access to the elements of the machine. Recognition of the work uniform and helmet allows to track that the worker is observing safety measures. Face recognition allows us to identify a person and check his competence to work with a specific machine. Determining the operator's presence in the hazardous area is a means of maintaining safety at the machine. Finding the distance between the operator and the elements of the machine allows us to determine the physical interaction with the machine.

The use of a multi-platform allows the operator to receive information on interaction with the machine without the necessary equipment on his smartphone and quickly prevent safety violations. The operator can view the list of current persons in the area of the machine for quick interaction with personnel.

Calculations are carried out on a central computer server, which is located near the machine. Fast data transfer and processing is ensured.

The operator receives a large number of basic events related to the presence of uniform elements, person identification, and distance determination. A composite event about the presence of the necessary uniform consists of the presence of a work uniform and a work helmet. Also, a composite event is the presence of a person in the danger zone without the necessary authority. This event consists of identifying persons, finding the distance, and information about the level of access and competence of a person.

C. Screen image text analysis from CNC display monitor to detect errors

Recognition of the CNC error code from the control panel screen allows us to receive errors that occurred during the operation of the machine in real-time without interfering with the operation of the system. The errors received are analyzed and the results are presented to the operator.

The use of a multi-platform allows us to interact with the system not only while at the work computer but also during absence from the workplace. The operator can receive information about the appeared and recognized the error in smartphone in the form of a PUSH notification, for a timely response and troubleshooting the equipment.

Computations for error recognition are carried out on an intermediate device when information is transmitted to the main computer server. Using the computing device directly next to the webcam will reduce the load on the central computing device.

The operator is presented with the last recognized error and history with time stamps. For each recognized error, a composite event is generated in which its description is shown with the methods for eliminating the error described in the official CNC manual. An event consisting of several errors is also a composite event. The operator is offered recommendations for their elimination, described by a person working with the machine. Providing the operator with analyzed data increases efficiency and reduces problem resolution time.

To deploy services, we need the installation of IP67, IP68 video cameras. The installation of protected cameras is required to prevent damage from dust and water exposure that can occur in a factory environment. The use of a twisted pair cable allows the camera to be powered via PoE (Power over Ethernet) and provides speeds up to 10 Mbps. A switch equipped with PoE ports is used for power supply. It is required to select the correct switch, since with a large number of connected cameras, the switch will not be able to provide enough power for all cameras.

D. Basic and composite events

The correct connection of all services to video devices for receiving data is provided by a user-defined config. The config includes network data for correct connection, authentication data for security, parameters of the received video stream, and the requirements for the video stream imposed by the service. The service results are saved in the MongoDB database.

Events:

- Events definition and specification: basic and composite events [21] [22].
- Composite events operators based on Snoop expressions.
- Table with examples of basic and composite events.

The event-driven data model allows us to organize interaction between software modules within the framework of a given application function. Software modules can be loosely coupled, i.e. to create a module, only the specification of the events to be processed with the rules for their inference is needed, which allows organizing a distributed microservice software infrastructure. Moreover, such a model allows us to combine heterogeneous data sources, forming a single consistent view with a high level of abstraction for a more accurate way of identifying events that occur.

An event in industrial equipment video monitoring systems is determined by a finite time interval at which some integral (indivisible) industrial phenomenon occurs, i.e. such a phenomenon either occurs entirely or does not occur at all. An industrial phenomenon occurs when the state is changed in the physical environment of an industrial enterprise. The environment is equipped with a video surveillance system that allows recording such events at a certain point in time.

In this case, an event occurring in the time interval between two consecutive points is considered to have occurred at the time of the endpoint of the interval.

At the initialization stage, it is necessary to describe the events that will be "tracked" based on video streams received from CCTV (Closed-circuit television) cameras. The following are suggested as basic rules: each video camera generates a separate video stream, which can contain many key elements (phenomena and anomalies) that make up a basic event. At the request of the developer, the underlying event can change depending on time, space, and context. The number of basic events from one video stream can be unlimited. Several video streams contain main events. Several major events make up a composite event (based on video streams $1 \ldots n$). A basic event depends on time, space, and context. Basic events can be independent and observed in different periods of time with different durations. Composite events can include several simple sequential or simultaneous basic events, as well as depend on other composite events. Composite events represent the end result, which can be presented in the form of a graph, diagram, text. The result, in turn, should be understandable and representative of the user.

Table I shows the composite events that result from the service. Composite events are made up of some basic and composite events functionality required by operators to service the machine.

The service for monitoring mechanical components monitors basic events: head type recognition, head rotation angle detection, shock detection. The composite head positioning event uses basic head type and angle detection events. For composite event tracking, the head type is determined based on its position in the storage rack and its external characteristics. The angle of rotation is tracked using visual elements on the head and displaceable when it is rotated. Tracking the correct positioning allows us to avoid breakdowns when installing the head on the machine since the machine does not check the current angle of rotation of the head and the installation is an automatic process of the machine and is little controlled by the operator. The tracking of counterweight installation depends on basic impact detection events and the type of head installed. Tracking the type of head installed allows us to know if a counterweight is needed on a given head. Impact tracking allows us to determine if the head is balanced. Installing a counterweight prevents incorrect machining of parts and is a necessary element for some machining heads.

The operator monitoring in the area of the machine monitors basic events: work uniform recognition, helmet recognition, human and face recognition, object distance detection. A composite event indicating that the operator is wearing appropriate clothing and protective equipment uses basic helmet and uniform recognition events. Every employee working in the plant must wear a special work uniform and be equipped with a helmet to protect the head. Wearing this uniform is required to comply with safety regulations and to save the life of employees. To track illegal access to the machine, human and face recognition events, object distance detection, as well as a database of employees with their competencies and access levels are used. Composing a composite event requires recognizing people's faces and distance to objects. If a person is in the service area, then his competence to work with this machine is checked. In a factory environment, with a large space and a large number of workers, it is required to control the level of access to equipment. It is required not to allow unqualified personnel to work with the machine without the participation of the machine operator. It is also required to track who at what time worked with the machine. The composite event of recognition of a person in a danger zone consists of human and face recognition, object distance detection. Recognition of a person and the distance to dangerous objects occurs, if the distance is less than a certain one, then the person is considered to be in the danger zone. An important element when working in a factory is compliance with safety measures; this can be solved by detecting a person in the hazardous area next to the machine in operation.

The screen image text analysis monitors a basic event - the appearance of error code on the screen. A composite event showing the operator a detailed description of the error consists of an error tracked on the screen and a database with a description of all available CNC errors. Obtaining a detailed description saves the operator from searching for information and provides information about the description and the method for resolving the error that has occurred. A composite event of related errors consists of several events of the occurrence of an error code at a time interval. It allows us to track errors that appear in a group for accurate identification of the malfunction and quick correction.

TABLE I. BASIC AND COMPOSITE EVENTS

Service	*Composite event*	*Basic event*	*Functionality*
Monitoring for position and movement of mechanical components	Correct head positioning	Head type recognition, head rotation angle detection	Prevention of breakage of parts of the head mounts, due to incorrect positioning of the head during its installation
	Counterweight Installation Requirements	Head type recognition, shock detection	Prevention of the appearance of defects on the object being processed by the machine, due to the appearance of vibration on the processing head
Monitoring for operator (human) presence in the area	Full uniform availability	Work uniform recognition, helmet recognition	Ensures the implementation of safety measures to protect the health of personnel
	Determining the access level	Human and face recognition, a database of employee qualifications and access levels, object distance detection	Prevention of access to personnel not qualified to operate the machine, to prevent damage due to poor quality maintenance
	Recognition of a person in a danger zone	Human and face recognition, object distance detection	Protection of personnel from being in hazardous areas where a person can be injured as a result of the operation of the machine
Monitoring for text messages observed on the equipment display	Error code with detailed description	Error code recognition, a database compiled from the official CNC error manual	Providing the operator with real-time error information, which will allow faster correction of errors and ensure the smooth operation of the machine
	Related errors	Recognition of error codes	Tracking error chains when a lot of errors appear, to accurately identify the problem and fix it as soon as possible

Table II shows the current capabilities of the service and possible improvements. Current capabilities refers to the capabilities that are currently provided by the installed services at the factory. Possible improvements refer to additional service capabilities that can be implemented to help workers and management.

TABLE II. SERVICE CABILITIES AND OPPORTUNITIES

Service	*Cabilities*	*Opportunities*
Monitoring mechanical components	Determining the angle of installation of the processing head and the type of installed head, as well as determining the installation of the counterweight	Recognition of the type of processing of parts in the working area
Operator presence in the area	Identification of a person in the danger zone and identification by face, the presence of a helmet and uniform	Tracking a worker's wearing a medical mask
Screen image text analysis	Error code recognition	Recognition of X Y Z coordinates published on the CNC screen

V. CONCLUSION

This paper discussed the service development problem of industrial video data analytics when services provide close to real-time assistance. We presented an edge-centric architecture for constructing such smart assistance services. Based on this architecture, we implemented several pilot services to demonstrate the opportunities of industrial video data analytics.

- Monitoring mechanical components of equipment to detect deviations in machine operations;
- Operator presence in the area to control production processes;
- Screen image text analysis from CNC display monitor to detect errors.

The services are deployed and experimented for monitoring industrial production equipment (technical state and its evolution, ongoing production processes, equipment operating conditions). Our early experiemnts show the high potential of edge-centric video data analitics for smart assistance in IIoT systems.

ACKNOWLEDGMENT

This research is implemented in Petrozavodsk State University (PetrSU) with financial support by the Ministry of Science and Higher Education of Russia within Agreement no. 075-11-2019-088 of 20.12.2019 on the topic "Creating the high-tech production of mobile microprocessor computing modules based on SiP and PoP technology for smart data collection, mining, and interaction with surrounding sources". The reported research study is supported by RFBR (research project # 19-07-01027). The work is implemented within the Government Program of Flagship University Development for Petrozavodsk State University (PetrSU) in 2017–2021.

REFERENCES

[1] D. Korzun, E. Balandina, A. Kashevnik, S. Balandin, and F. Viola, Ambient Intelligence Services in IoT Environments: Emerging Research and Opportunities. IGI Global, 2019.

[2] K. Schoeffmann, M. A. Hudelist, and J. Huber, "Video interaction tools: A survey of recent work," ACM Computing Surveys (CSUR), vol. 48, no. 14, Sep 2015.

[3] Y. Chen, Y. Xie, Y. Hu, Y. Liu, and G. Shou, "Design and implementation of video analytics system based on edge computing," in 2018 International Conference on Cyber-Enabled Distributed Computing and Knowledge Discovery (CyberC), 2018, pp. 130–137.

[4] N. Anand, A. Chintalapally, C. Puri, and T. Tung, "Practical edge analytics: Architectural approach and use cases," in 2017 IEEE International Conference on Edge Computing (EDGE), 2017, pp. 236–239.

[5] N. Bazhenov and D. Korzun, "Event-driven video services for monitoring in edge-centric internet of things environments," in Proc. 25th Conf. Open Innovations Association FRUCT, Nov. 2019, pp. 47–56.

[6] K. Yeow, A. Gani, R. W. Ahmad, J. J. P. C. Rodrigues, and K. Ko, "Decentralized consensus for edge-centric internet of things: A review, taxonomy, and research issues," IEEE Access, vol. 6, 2018, pp. 1513–1524.

[7] D. Wu, J. Yan, H. Wang, and R. Wang, "User-centric edge sharing mechanism in software-defined ultra-dense networks," IEEE Journal on Selected Areas in Communications, vol. 38, no. 7, 2020, pp. 1531–1541.

[8] E. Kim, "Smart city service platform associated with smart home," in 2017 International Conference on Information Networking (ICOIN), 2017, pp. 608–610.

[9] M. A. Fabrício, F. H. Behrens, and D. Bianchini, "Monitoring of industrial electrical equipment using iot," IEEE Latin America Transactions, vol. 18, no. 08, 2020, pp. 1425–1432.

[10] A. Rastegari, A. Archenti, and M. Mobin, "Condition based maintenance of machine tools: Vibration monitoring of spindle units," 01 2017.

[11] W. Tao, Z.-H. Lai, M. C. Leu, and Z. Yin, "Worker activity recognition in smart manufacturing using imu and semg signals with convolutional neural networks," Procedia Manufacturing, vol. 26, 2018, pp. 1159 – 1166, 46th SME North American Manufacturing Research Conference, NAMRC 46, Texas, USA. [Online]. Available: http://www.sciencedirect.com/science/article/pii/S235197891830828X

[12] M. Darji, J. Dave, N. Asif, C. Godawat, V. Chudasama, and K. Upla, "Licence plate identification and recognition for non-helmeted motorcyclists using light-weight convolution neural network," in 2020 International Conference for Emerging Technology (INCET), 2020, pp. 1–6.

[13] S. Shetty, A. S. Devadiga, S. S. Chakkaravarthy, and K. A. V. Kumar, "Ote-ocr based text recognition and extraction from video frames," in 2014 IEEE 8th International Conference on Intelligent Systems and Control (ISCO), 2014, pp. 229–232.

[14] P. L. Venetianer and H. Deng, "Performance evaluation of an intelligent video surveillance system – a case study," Computer Vision and Image Understanding, vol. 114, no. 11, 2010, pp. 1292 – 1302, special issue on Embedded Vision.

[15] C. Stergiou, K. E. Psannis, A. P. Plageras, G. Kokkonis, and Y. Ishibashi, "Architecture for security monitoring in iot environments," in 2017 IEEE 26th International Symposium on Industrial Electronics (ISIE), 2017, pp. 1382–1385.

[16] P. Gokhale and S. Singh, "Multi-platform strategies, approaches and challenges for developing mobile applications," in 2014 International Conference on Circuits, Systems, Communication and Information Technology Applications (CSCITA), 2014, pp. 289–293.

[17] M. K. et al., "Hybrid software development approaches in practice: A european perspective," IEEE Software, vol. 36, no. 4, 2019, pp. 20–31.

[18] N. Harth and C. Anagnostopoulos, "Edge-centric efficient regression analytics," in 2018 IEEE International Conference on Edge Computing (EDGE), 2018, pp. 93–100.

[19] H. Wei, L. Gui, and F. Li, "A review of shock detection technology based on embedded system," in 2013 25th Chinese Control and Decision Conference (CCDC), 2013, pp. 2336–2341.

[20] N. Bazhenov and D. Korzun, "Smart video services based on edge computing with multiple cameras," in Proc. 26th Conf. Open Innovations Association FRUCT, Apr. 2020, pp. 485–490.

[21] S. Chakravarthy and D. Mishra, "Snoop: An expressive event specification language for active databases," Data & Knowledge Engineering, vol. 14, no. 1, 1994, pp. 1 – 26.

[22] R. Adaikkalavan and S. Chakravarthy, "Snoopib: Interval-based event specification and detection for active databases," Data & Knowledge Engineering, vol. 59, no. 1, 2006, pp. 139 – 165.

Automated Code Generation of Multi-Agent Interaction for Constructing Semantic Services

Sergei A. Marchenkov

Department of Computer Science
Petrozavodsk State University (PetrSU)
Petrozavodsk, Russia
e-mail: marchenk@cs.petrsu.ru

***Abstract*—This paper proposes a solution to the problem of simplifying the development and maintenance of smart space applications by creating tools for automated code generation of multi-agent interaction for constructing semantic services. The general scheme of automated code generation process of multi-agent interaction for constructing semantic services is introduced. By expanding the Web Ontology Language for Services (OWL-S), a unified ontological description of the semantics of service constructing processes is introduced. The code generation procedures for agent data object model and interaction processes are presented. The efforts, in automated development of semantic services through the use of the proposed unified service ontology ,and the code generator are investigated based on estimation of time to generate program code and the quality metrics of generated code.**

Keywords–semantic services; code generation; ontology-driven development; information-driven interaction.

I. Introduction

The Smart Spaces (SmS) approach to smart application development combines Internet of Things technologies with the Semantic Web to create a class of ubiquitous environments [1]. The smart nature of this approach is due to the need to provide participants in SmS with services in the conditions of their mass use, the presence of heterogeneity of computing devices and software components, their physical distribution, a variety of resources used and possible means of network communications for transferring data between participants. The interaction participants are software agents, who are consumers and producers of shared information storage.

Each agent in SmS application works in accordance with a specific domain area and model of information-driven interaction with other agents in the process of constructing and delivering services [2]. The agent logic developer uses the Application Programming Interface (API) middleware to access SmS information storage. From the point of view of agents, information storage is organized as an Resource Description Framework (RDF) graph, as a rule, in accordance with some ontology defined using the Web Ontology Language (OWL) description language.

SmS middleware (platform) is a software layer that allows agents to share content. A middleware supports a variety of semantic interoperable access primitives, including ontology-oriented ones. Currently, there are many available software implementations of platforms for creating such SmS: OpenIoT [3], Neo4j [4], SEPA [5], FIESTA-IoT [6]. As an example, the paper discusses the CuteSIB [7] platform using an ontology-oriented approach to service development. The environments of the smart museum [8] and collaborative work [9] environments are considered as examples of applications.

The construction of services in SmS is implemented as a distributed computing process, that allows creating more complex system solutions based on information-driven interaction of agents. In other words, services are created as a result of agents working together. Such agents perform a step-by-step process of changing the shared information storage based on "publish/subscribe" models in order to implement the application function and ensure interaction with the resources of the computing environment. The consumers of services are often users. Therefore, the process of knowledge extraction and service delivery, as a rule, is personalized taking into account the priorities and preferences of users, considered in the context of the current situation and the state of the environment.

The elaboration on the Semantic Web concept and related concepts, such as Web 3.0 [10] and the Semantic Web of Things [11], defines the direction for the elaboration on SmS services towards semantic services. The description of a semantic service is represented by a machine-interpreted service ontology. SmS services can be defined as semantic services, which must have uniquely described semantics, be available among other heterogeneous environments, be suitable for automated search, composition, proactive construction and proactive delivery. The use of semantic services in the SmS approach changes the requirements for the development of services, and therefore, SmS applications. In connection with the constantly growing and dynamically changing set of participants in the SmS environment, the complexity of the phases of development and maintenance of services increases.

Unified service ontology. The design of semantic services should be based on a general unified ontology. Such an ontology defines not only the service interface in terms of transmitted data and return values, but also defines the purpose of the service, describes the process of its construction, and uniquely determines its semantics. With this consistent design approach, the services of different SmS applications can interact with each other regardless of the domain area and environment. Providing in this way the network interaction of the SmS environments, it is possible to achieve the integration of both the SmS themselves and their applications for solving collaborative tasks based on semantic services.

Automation of agent programming processes. The way to develop applications is needed that allows to reduce the amount of program code generated by an application developer during routine tasks through the use of computer-aided design and programming tools. In particular, the automation of agent programming processes when constructing services can be achieved through the use of semantic service ontologies. Ontologies are accepted as input parameters to generate an object model and code templates for object-oriented programming languages. By understanding the semantics of the service, as well as information about the available resources of the environment, ontology-based self-organization of agents can be achieved by defining their functional roles, interaction models and operations/functions in the process of constructing and delivering a service.

The paper proposes a solution to the problem of simplifying the development and maintenance of SmS applications by creating tools for automated code generation of multi-agent interaction for constructing semantic services.

The rest of the paper is organized as follows. Section II introduces the general scheme of automated code generation process of multi-agent interaction for constructing semantic services. Section III provides the ontology of semantic service in SmS. Section IV proposes the code generation procedures for agent data object model and interaction processes. Section V evaluates the developer efforts in automated development of semantic services through the use of the proposed unified service ontology and the code generator. Finally, Section VI concludes the paper.

II. Automatic Ontology-Driven Development

The development of SmS applications follows the principles of ontology-driven software development. According to these principles, the design phase is reduced to the creation of a specification for a specific domain and services in the form of an OWL/RDF description. The use of ontologies allows to achieve a common understanding of the structure of information storage between agents to facilitate knowledge reuse through concepts already defined in other ontologies, as well as support for formal logic and logical reasoning [12]. Thus, it is beneficial to use the features of the ontology-driven approach in the case of using ontologies at all phases of development.

To automate the development stages, traditional design and development methods are being replaced by methods that facilitate the implementation of an approach with extensive use of Computer-Aided Design (CAD) and Computer-Aided Programming (CAP) tools. Such tools support application prototyping.

CAD tools are are being used to automate processes aimed at creating and maintaining various ontological and graphical representations during of application systems design. In turn, CAP tools are being used to simplify the task of programming agents. Rather than directly coding up executable programs for software agents, the developer provides an ontology with a problem domain and service specification allowing code generation algorithms to create correct code functions, data structures, and other elements of the specified programming language. The integrating efforts of CAD and CAP tools will bring automated program-code generation directly from design-phase specifications. CAD and CAP tools can also be distributed together with a middleware providing an integrated environment for building/deploying and managing applications, such as in the OpenIoT middleware [3].

The design phase is reduced to creating a specification of a problem domain and services as an RDF/OWL description. There is a large number of works aimed at solving CAD problems at the design phase for ontology-driven software development [12][13]. For example, ontology development tools, such as Protégé [14] and OWL-S Editor [15] allow users to create these specifications and provide guidance to find mistakes based on validation mechanisms. These tools serve as rapid prototyping environments, in which ontology designers can instantly create individuals of their ontology and experiment with semantic restrictions, and enable developers to visualize descriptions in a graphical manner are even able to generate user interfaces that can be further customized for knowledge acquisition in a particular domain.

At the implementation phase, which involves the use of programming languages to encode the resulting design solutions, software agents from the design specifications and models are created. At this phase, solving the CAP tool [16] is not enough for an automated task of ontology-driven programming of agents. Existing solutions for ontology-driven software development solve this problem in part by mapping OWL classes, their instances and properties to programming language classes, their objects, and fields, respectively [14].

Obviously, this approach is difficult both for practical implementation and for use in the case of statically typed compiled programming languages. However, it is convenient for dynamically typed interpreted and object-oriented programming languages. This approach is primarily intended for creating data structures and elements of the object model of an agent problem domain. However, it does not allow creating methods, functions and other elements of internal program logic. One of the examples of this approach is SmartSlog CodeGen, which is part of the SmatSlog ontology library designed for creating SmS applications. Its mechanisms allow creating data structures for particular OWL ontology entities.

A solution is proposed, aimed at creating the program code generator for agents based on ontology using object-oriented programming languages (e.g., C++, Java, Python). The general scheme of the program code generation process is shown in Figure 1. The main features of the proposed code generation scheme are: (i) use as input ontologies, together with OWL domain ontologies, service ontologies for SmS based on the OWL-S ontology [15]; (ii) generation, in addition to data structures, elements of the program logic of agent interaction based on the API of the SmS middleware for the purpose of constructing and delivering services, as well as an object model of the domain.

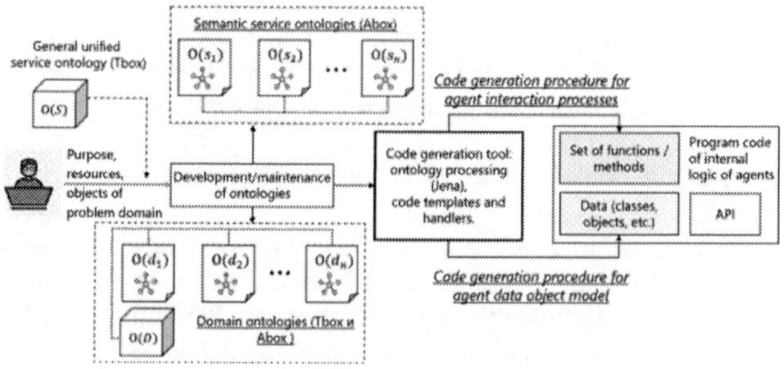

Figure 1. The general scheme of automated code generation process of multi-agent interaction

An agent developer provides a problem domain specification as an OWL description and a specification of SmS services as an OWL-S-based description. The generator uses a static pattern of templates and handlers. Code templates are "pre-code" of data structures, classes and functions that implement OWL-S-based and OWL ontologies entities and their properties.Handlers can transform one or more templates into the final code replacing specialized tags with names and elements taken from ontologies. The code can be generated for several agents, depending on the agents involved in constructing and delivering the services described with the OWL-S-based specification. The transformation should occur during ontology RDF graph traversal based on Jena OWL framework. Jena constructs a meta-model to represent the graph. The generator should traverse this model comprehensively, and those nodes are visited that a handler needs to transform its templates into final code.

III. Ontological Semantic Services Model

SmS allow effectively organizing the interaction of its participants and their sharing of information [1]. In particular, a virtual digital image is created for each participant, which is semantically linked with other participants and resources. The service ontology describes the context of the environment and its participants, interacting agents and the resources involved. The ontological model is created on the basis of a conceptual description of semantic web services using models for organizing information-driven interaction of agents, defined within the SmS approach. Due to such a unified ontological description of service construction processes, an increase in the quality of service design is achieved. Services become suitable for automated search, composition, construction and delivery to users by describing the interface (service purpose, inputs and outputs, etc.) and the processes that occur.

The World Wide Web Consortium (W3C) has introduced an ontology built on top of OWL to describe semantic web services. This ontology is called OWL-S [17]. The main purpose of OWL-S is to allow users to discover, invoke, compose, and monitor with a high degree of automation Web resources offering particular services and having particular properties,using a minimalistic approach for describing semantic Web Services. OWL-S describes the characteristics of a service by using three top-level concepts: a service profile, a service model, and a service grounding.

The purpose of a service profile is to define a service in a uniform way for future use, detailing the content of queries and conditions under which specific results will occur, and, if necessary, step-by-step processes leading to these results. The process model describes how to access a service and what happens when the service is executed. The service process model describes a service as a collection of atomic and composite processes. An atomic process corresponds to a "one-step" procedure that takes input parameters, processes them, and then returns a result. Composite processes decompose into other processes; by defining their decomposition using control constructs (for example, *If-Then-Else*, *Split*, *Repeat-While*). The service grounding defines how the service is invoked by the consumer of the service, including the communication protocol and message format. In the case of the M3 architecture [18], the service foundation ontology is an optional part, since the interaction of agents is organized using the Smart Space Access Protocol (SSAP) protocol, which does not require a separate description.

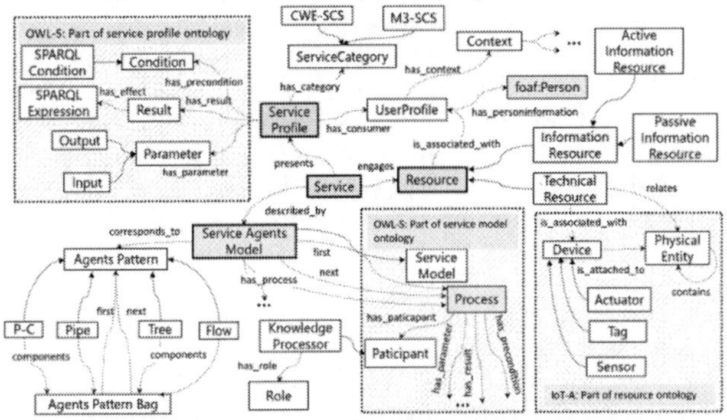

Figure 2. Ontological model of semantic service in SmS.

A unified ontological description of the service semantics for SmS is proposed, containing a set of terminological axioms (see Figure 2). A service profile describes a service using Inputs, Outputs, Preconditions, Effects (IOPEs). The *has_output* property is used to represent the output from a service resource to a consumer. If a service needs to specify input data for processing by a resource or control action in the form of notifications, then this is determined using the *has_input* property.

The initial state of the shared information storage for initializing the process of constructing a service is set using a precondition (*has_precondition*). The desired state of the storage is determined using the resulting condition (*has_result*). Preconditions and results are specified using expressions. There are several possible approaches that allow using rules and logic for the RDF/OWL view [19]. The main idea is to treat expressions as literals using Protocol and RDF Query Language (SPARQL) expressions, which are defined using the SPARQL-Expression class.

The *has_category* property describes service categories based on SmS service categories. Categories are determined based on criteria, such as impact, underlying resource, way of integration, function performed. The category defines a typical model of information-driven interaction of agents [1].

OWL-S ontology is very flexible, but OWL-S solutions are not enough to use it fully to describe the semantics of a SmS service. In order to take into account the priorities and preferences of users (if the customer is a human being) providing the personification of a service, the existing service profile is expanded by the *has_consumer* property and its *UserProfile* class object, which is described both in terms of user contextual information. Such information reflects the state of the user's computing environment (*has_context*), as well as his preferences, interests, personal information represented by part of the Friend of a Friend (FOAF) ontology (*has_personinformation*). The OWL-S ontology also does not support a multi-agent approach for describing a service process model. The vision of agents in the OWL-S ontology is reduced: agents are considered primarily as consumers or "seekers" of services. At the same time, the process of constructing a service in the SmS approach is a process of interaction of several agents.

The service process ontology is extended by introducing the *ServiceAgentsModel* class to describe the process of constructing services for SmS. The process is described by a model of information-driven interaction of agents, which is determined depending on the service category. The interaction of each agent (*KnowledgeProccessor*), represented as an extension of the participant's class, is determined by its functional role (*has_role* property) performed in the model. A functional role is an abstract description of the functional properties of an agent. The role of the agent defines the general principles of implementation of the individual internal logic of the agent, as well as the principles of interaction with other agents. The logic of a separate agent leads to the interaction of agents during the construction of a service based on interaction patterns (*AgentsPattern*) described using such architectural abstractions as Provider-Consumer (PC), Pipe, Tree, Flow. The process of interaction between agents can consist of several patterns presented in a certain sequence (*AgentsPatternBag*).

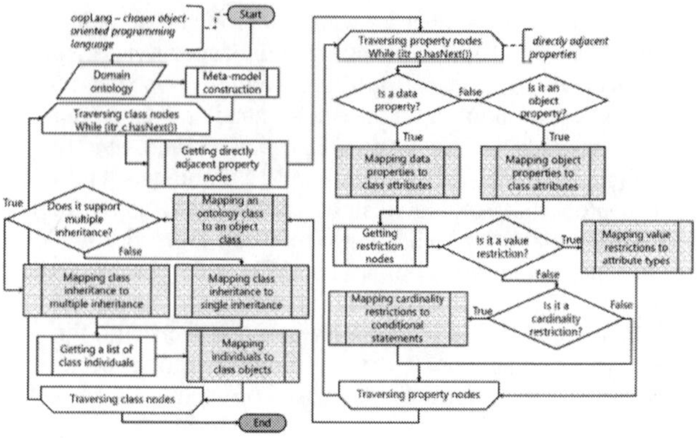

Figure 3. The code generation procedure for an agent data object model.

IV. Automating Programming of Multi-agent Interaction based on Code Generation

The automation of programming processes for agents involved in constructing and delivering services is achieved through the use of a program code generator. As a result of the design stage of SmS application, the developer has a set of ontologies, which are divided into two groups: (1) the domain ontology and (2) the service ontology for SmS based on OWL-S. Ontologies provide the necessary semantics that are used to generate code in object-oriented programming languages. The generator uses algorithms for automating agent programming processes to implement the structures of the object model and for the agents interaction. The code generation procedure for an agent data object model takes the domain ontology as an input parameter. The code generation procedure for agent interaction processes takes as an input parameter the service ontology to generate blocks of agent program code.

The object model merges data and functionality into an abstract variable type – an object. The object model provides a more realistic representation of objects that the end user can more easily understand. While an ontology structure contains definitions of concepts (classes) and relationship between concepts and attributes (properties, aspects, parameters), an object model uses classes to represent objects and functions to model relationships of objects and the attributes. The similarity of concepts in an ontology with an object model determines the applicability of an object-oriented approach to ontology modeling. However, ontology represents a more richer information model than Java objects by supporting such distinctive features as inheritance of properties, symmetric/transitive/inverse properties, full multiple inheritances among classes and properties [20].

The code generation procedure for an agent data object model is presented in the flowchart (see Figure. 3). he main idea of the ontology-object mapping is to create a set of classes and objects in such a way that each ontological class with their instances, properties, slots, and facets has its equivalent in the structures of an object-oriented programming language.

Constructing SmS service can be viewed as a set of calls to agents' software functions. The service ontology for SmS based on OWL-S provides a declarative, computer-interpreted description that includes the semantics of the IOPEs model that must be specified for each process. The process entity can be used to generate procedures, functions and other elements of the target programming language that implement information-driven interaction and the necessary internal logic of agents. The code generation procedure for agent interaction processes in the flowchart is shown in Figure 4.

Instances of the *AtomicProcces* class are used to generate function code. The *rdf:ID* attribute of the AtomicProcess class defines the function name. Each *has_input* property with *rdf:ID* attribute corresponds to the input parameters of the function. The type of the input parameter can be obtained by extracting at the *parameter_type* property.

The functions internal logic is implemented using SPARQL queries and sets of program statements. The *has_precondition* property with a SPARQL expression defines a precondition code block that describes the initial state of the information storage. A precondition block is required to initialize the service construction. A code block is generated that calls the API middleware (SmS platform) to execute a SPARQL query (usually an ASK query) and verifies the query result using an "if-then-else" statement. A similar generation process is performed for a code block representing a result condition (*has_result*) — a set of actions performed at the end of a function call.

The *has_output* property with the *parameter_type* property corresponds to the output parameter and defines the function return value. The required data types (string, unsignedLong, etc.) are described using an XML Schema Definition (XSD) schema. Elements of the object model can be used as input and output parameters. The *CompositeProcess* class, by analogy with a composite process, defines a function that calls other functions within itself, which are described by *CompositeProcess* or *AtomicProcess* entities. In this case, calls to internal functions can be specified using control constructs (*If-Then-Else*, *Repeat-While*, etc.) which can be transformed into the corresponding statements of the programming language.

An instance of the ServiceAgentsModel class is used by agents to define their role in the process of constructing and delivering services, as well as a method of information-driven interaction based on the publish subscribe model. For this purpose, in advance, in the code of each agent a block is formed with the necessary subscription operations using internal functions, handlers, and API functions. Each subscription operation query is specified by a SPARQL query that can be obtained from the *has_subprecondition* property, where a subscription expression is specified using SPARQL queries that use domain classes and properties. In addition,

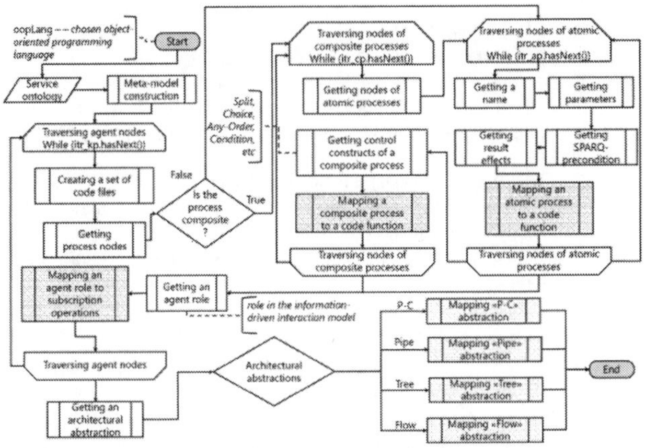

Figure 4. The code generation procedure for agent interaction processes.

subscription operations can be defined based on the execution results of agent processes defined in the *Result* classes. Each such class defines what domain changes are produced during the execution of an agent. During the execution of agents, their self-organization can occur as each agent is aware of its purpose in the interaction model based on interaction patterns (*AgentsPattern* class).

V. Effort Estimation

Efficiency is the relationship between the results achieved, and the resources used. Efficiency of the proposed solutions is determined on the basis of effort estimation in automated development of semantic services through the use of the unified service ontology and the generator of the agent interaction program code. For effort estimation, any unit of measurement of the duration of ongoing processes can be used. The effort in semantic service development are considered in two phases: design and implementation.

The main stages in a design phase of multi-agent software systems are:

1) defining the roles of agents and their functional description;
2) conceptual modelling of inter-role interaction based on the selected protocol;
3) modelling the interaction between the user and the system, and defining the access interface;
4) creating the code structure for each agent and the system as a whole.

The use of the proposed solutions by the developer makes it possible to fix the obtained design decisions (agent roles, protocol and model of agent interaction, service interface) while directly creating an ontological description of services in unified terms. It is known that the use of ontologies at the design phase increases the developer's efforts to create design solutions. However, some additional efforts can be minimized, while others provide additional opportunities at the next development phases (e.g., programming automation, agents self-organization). One way to minimize efforts is to use existing computer-aided design tools (such as Protégé), which provide a software environment for rapid prototyping.

Additional design efforts allow obtaining uniform service ontologies that define the interaction interface and describe the execution semantics. With this unified design approach, services across domains can interact with each other independently of the computing environment. The use of the solutions is not limited to the design phase. The service ontologies are used to automate further service programming processes (creating an object model, code functions).

TABLE I. Proportion of generated code for services.

Service	Agents and their roles		Object data model		Information-driven interaction		Internal logic		Total	
			SLOC	%	SLOC	%	SLOC	%	SLOC	%
User presence and activity service (S_{prs})	Presence processor adapter-agent	all	26	8,8	78	26,4	191	64,8	295	100
		gen.	21	7,1	40	13,6	9	3	**70**	**23,7**
	Presence detector aggregator-agent	all	18	11,2	44	27,5	98	61,2	160	100
		gen.	14	8,7	18	11,3	5	2,8	**37**	**23,1**
	Activity monitor-agent	all	74	13,2	88	15,7	392	71,1	560	100
		gen.	52	9,3	75	13,4	13	2,3	**140**	**25**
Historical data enrichment service (S_{enr})	External finder-agent	all	65	9,6	162	23,9	451	66,5	678	100
		gen.	50	7,4	103	15,2	7	1	**160**	**23,6**
	Semantic controller-agent	all	222	12,6	515	29,2	1028	58,2	1765	100
		gen.	148	8,4	339	19,2	23	1,3	**510**	**28,9**
	Enrichment aggregator-agent	all	391	11,9	898	27,3	2001	60,8	3290	100
		gen.	296	9	513	15,6	26	0,8	**835**	**25,4**

Programming effort is investigated based on the ratio of the total number of lines of agent source code to that automatically generated using the proposed implementation of the program code generator for the following service: user presence and activity service (S_{prs}) and historical data enrichment service (S_{enr}). Table I provides the percentage of generated program code for agents involved in the implementation of services. The program code, regardless of the role of the software agent, consists of the following blocks:

1) structures of the object data model and methods for working with them;
2) information-driven interaction based on supported operations for middleware;
3) internal logic, including local processing of general information.

The average share of generated program code was 23.4%, with the greatest results falling on the "information-driven interaction" block. For the object data model, the generator also shows high rates, the average coverage percentage of the corresponding source code with the generated code is 68%.

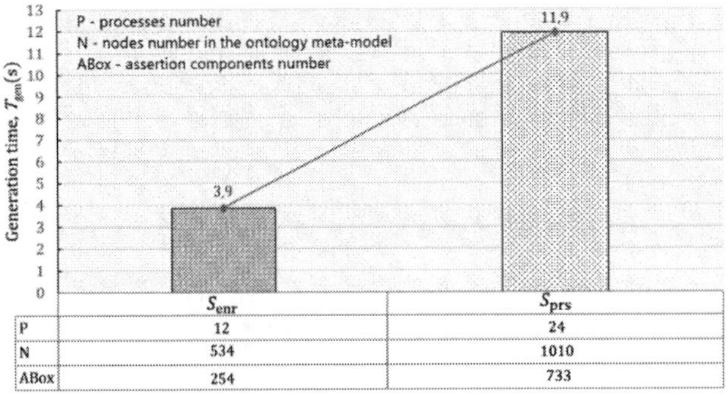

Figure 5. Time to generate program code for service implementations.

The process of programming services imposes additional efforts associated with the time spent on the process of generating program code. The generator accepts the developed service ontologies and the domain ontology as input parameters. The generation time of the program code depends on ontological metrics (cyclomatic complexity, vocabulary size) that characterize the complexity of traversing the ontology meta-model (ontological graph). Experiments have shown (see Figure 5) that when processing the ontology for the user presence and activity service (S_{prs}), which has the highest metrics from the developed ontologies, the time for traversing the meta-model and generating code does not exceed 12 s.

TABLE II. QUALITY METRICS OF GENERATED CODE.

Metric	*Value*
Total number of generated code lines	**49**
Cyclomatic complexity	**4**
Number of distinct operators: η_1	13
Number of distinct operands: η_2	17
Total number of occurrences of operators: N_1	26
Total number of occurrences of operands: N_2	41
Halstead vocabulary: $\eta = \eta_1 + \eta_2$	30
Halstead program length: $N = N_1 + N_2$	67
Program volume: $V = N * \log_2 \eta$	406
Program difficulty: $D = \frac{\eta_1}{2} * \frac{N_2}{\eta_2}$	15.67
Programming effort: $E = D * V$	6362
Programming time (seconds): $T = \frac{E}{18}$	**353.5**

The quality of the generated code is investigated on the basis of calculating and evaluating the quality metrics of the code. The following quality metrics of the generated program code are measured: cyclomatic complexity and Halstead's metrics [21]. The measured metrics made it possible to estimate: the complexity of maintaining the generated code, efforts to create the code manually. Table II shows the measured metrics for one simple process of S_{prs} service. The cyclomatic complexity is 4, the estimated time to create such a code manually is 353.5 seconds.

VI. CONCLUSION

This paper proposed a solution to the problem of simplifying the development and maintenance of smart space applications by creating tools for automated code generation of multi-agent interaction for constructing semantic services. The general scheme of automated code generation process of multi-agent interaction for constructing semantic services was introduced. By expanding the OWL-S ontology, a unified ontological description of the semantics of service constructing processes was introduced. The code generation procedures for agent data object model and interaction processes were presented. The efforts in automated development of semantic services were investigated based on estimation of time to generate and the quality metrics of generated code.

ACKNOWLEDGMENT

The reported research study is supported by RFBR (research project # 19-07-01027). The work is implemented within the Government Program of Flagship University Development for Petrozavodsk State University (PetrSU) in 2017–2021.

REFERENCES

[1] D. G. Korzun, S. I. Balandin, A. M. Kashevnik, A. V. Smirnov, and A. V. Gurtov, "Smart spaces-based application development: M3 architecture, design principles, use cases, and evaluation," International Journal of Embedded and Real-Time Communication Systems (IJERTCS), vol. 8, no. 2, 2017, pp. 66–100.

[2] D. Korzun, "On the smart spaces approach to semantic-driven design of service-oriented information systems," in International Baltic Conference on Databases and Information Systems. Springer, 2016, pp. 181–195.

[3] J. Soldatos et al., "Openiot: Open source internet-of-things in the cloud," in Interoperability and Open-Source Solutions for the Internet of Things. Springer International Publishing, 2015, pp. 13–25.

[4] J. Guia, V. G. Soares, and J. Bernardino, "Graph databases: Neo4j analysis." in ICEIS (1), 2017, pp. 351–356.

[5] L. Roffia et al., "Dynamic linked data: A sparql event processing architecture," Future Internet, vol. 10, no. 4, 2018, p. 36.

[6] J. Lanza et al., "A proof-of-concept for semantically interoperable federation of iot experimentation facilities," Sensors, vol. 16, no. 7, 2016, p. 1006.

[7] I. Galov, A. Lomov, and D. Korzun, "Design of semantic information broker for localized computing environments in the Internet of Things," in Proc. 17th Conf. of Open Innovations Association FRUCT. IEEE, Apr. 2015, pp. 36–43.

[8] D. Korzun, S. Yalovitsyna, and V. Volokhova, "Smart services as cultural and historical heritage information assistance for museum visitors and personnel," Baltic Journal of Modern Computing, vol. 6, no. 4, 2018, pp. 418–433.

[9] S. A. Marchenkov, A. S. Vdovenko, and D. G. Korzun, "Enhancing the opportunities of collaborative work in an intelligent room using e-tourism services," Trudy SPIIRAN, vol. 50, 2017, pp. 165–189.

[10] A. Gyrard, M. Serrano, and G. A. Atemezing, "Semantic web methodologies, best practices and ontology engineering applied to internet of things," in 2015 IEEE 2nd World Forum on Internet of Things (WF-IoT), 2015, pp. 412–417.

[11] P. Kujur and B. Chhetri, "Evolution of world wide web: Journey from web 1.0 to web 4.0," International Journal of Computer Science and Technology, vol. 6, Jan. 2015.

[12] C. W. Yang, V. Dubinin, and V. Vyatkin, "Ontology driven approach to generate distributed automation control from substation automation design," IEEE Transactions on Industrial Informatics, vol. 13, no. 2, Feb. 2017, pp. 668–679.

[13] S. Isotani, I. I. Bittencourt, E. F. Barbosa, D. Dermeval, and R. O. A. Paiva, "Ontology driven software engineering: a review of challenges and opportunities," IEEE Latin America Transactions, vol. 13, no. 3, 2015, pp. 863–869.

[14] H. Knublauch, "Ontology-driven software development in the context of the semantic web: An example scenario with Protege/OWL," in 1st International workshop on the model-driven semantic web (MDSW2004), 2004, pp. 381–401.

[15] D. Elenius et al., "The owl-s editor–a development tool for semantic web services," in European Semantic Web Conference. Springer, 2005, pp. 78–92.

[16] A. Lomov, "Ontology-based kp development for smart-m3 applications," in 2013 13th Conference of Open Innovations Association (FRUCT). IEEE, 2013, pp. 94–100.

[17] D. Martin et al., "Bringing semantics to web services with owl-s," World Wide Web, vol. 10, no. 3, 2007, pp. 243–277.

[18] J. Honkola, H. Laine, R. Brown, and O. Tyrkkö, "Smart-M3 information sharing platform," in Proc. IEEE Symp. Computers and Communications (ISCC'10). IEEE Computer Society, Jun. 2010, pp. 1041–1046.

[19] E. Sirin, B. Parsia, B. C. Grau, A. Kalyanpur, and Y. Katz, "Pellet: A practical owl-dl reasoner," Journal of Web Semantics, vol. 5, no. 2, 2007, pp. 51–53.

[20] D. N. Batanov and W. Vongdoiwang, Using Ontologies to Create Object Model for Object-Oriented Software Engineering. Boston, MA: Springer US, 2007, pp. 461–487.

[21] T. Hariprasad, G. Vidhyagaran, K. Seenu, and C. Thirumalai, "Software complexity analysis using halstead metrics," in 2017 International Conference on Trends in Electronics and Informatics (ICEI). IEEE, 2017, pp. 1109–1113.

Status-aware and SLA-aware QoS Routing Model for SDN Transport Network

Atefeh Meshinchi
Polytechnique Montréal
Montreal, Canada
email: atefeh.meshinchi@polymtl.ca

Ranwa Al Mallah
Ryerson University
Montreal, Canada
email: ranwa.almallah@ryerson.ca

Alejandro Quintero
Polytechnique Montréal
Montreal, Canada
email: alejandro.quintero@polymtl.ca

***Abstract*—Internet of Things (IoT) is a key technological enabler to create smart environments and provide various benefits. In the context of a smart city, a huge number of IoT applications are being developed for emergency management operation and city traffic congestion management. These applications require fast system reaction to get the valuable data and make appropriate decisions. Therefore, it is essential to design and develop a service model that ensures an appropriate level of Quality of Service (QoS) for such applications. In this paper, we take advantage of Software-Defined Networking (SDN) technology integrated into the IoT system to propose a new QoS routing model for core transport SDN. In the model, the application QoS preferences and network elements status are directly considered in the resource allocation process aiming to satisfy the application expectation while maximizing network performance. We modeled a status-aware and Service-Level-Agreement-aware (SLA-aware) routing mechanism and implemented multi-path and load-balancing approaches in the model to enhance the network throughput and increase system availability.**

Keywords–Internet of Things; Routing; Quality of service; Software-Defined Networking.

I. INTRODUCTION

The proliferation of devices in a communicating–actuating network creates the Internet of Things (IoT). It is a radical evolution of the current Internet into a network of interconnected objects. In IoT, smart objects are able to sense, communicate, compute, analyze, and make nonhuman-intervention decisions using locally- or globally-gathered data. Diverse technologies and techniques in the field of devices, data, and communication are contributed to the fulfillment of the IoT services.

In the multi-layered IoT reference architecture [1], application and service support layers, also called middle-ware layer, interact directly with user requirements while the network layer transmits the data to the upper layer. The device layer provides the data collection capability. Quality of Service (QoS) management in IoT systems is a very complex task because of the extremely large variety of devices and services, as well as the technologies and techniques involved in the systems architecture.

Applications are fundamental to the IoT. They provide the presentation layer for the data captured from the billions of devices around the world. IoT application could be classified from different perspectives such as the type of information they manage, the type of recipient (person or system oriented), and their critically. In general, IoT applications are classified into three different types: (1) control applications, also called mission-critical applications,such as city-traffic management and emergency management, which need very fast response with as less error as possible, (2) monitoring applications, such as intelligent security surveillance tasks, which are fed by cameras and need more throughput, and (3) analysis and inquiry applications, such as the inquiry into the transported item state in the intelligent logistics, which are throughput and delay tolerant. Although other metrics enforced from device layer like quality of information and data sampling rate are important in the service quality, the productivity and performance of an IoT application is mainly impacted by the performance of the communication network.

The Internet as a large-scale networking system has had great success in the interconnection of computer networks and with the creation of IPv6 it extends the TCP/IP address spaces to provide identifiers for the large number of connected devices. However, the legacy computer network and the Internet still face some limitations. On one hand, the control intelligence, which is implemented by various routing and management protocols, is embedded in every network elements and It is difficult to change. Vendor-dependent platforms and interfaces make the Internet evolution complex and slow.

On the other hand, the Internet provides best-effort services and it may not meet the more specific requirements of applications in terms of service quality [2] [3]. Two main standardized QoS implementation models in classical IP networks are Integrated Services (IntServ) [4], with the idea of per-flow resource reservation, and Differentiated Services (DiffServ) [5], with the idea of traffic classification and prioritization. While both models are offering advanced features in traffic engineering, the scalability and robustness of the IntServ approach and lack of end-to-end connection guarantee and per-flow QoS setup in DiffServ are the drawbacks of the two approaches.

IPv6 as the most recent version of the Internet protocol (IP), resolve IPv4 depletion problem and bring more scalability for IP based solutions, particularly in the IoT domain where a large number of the devices/things interconnect with each other. IPv6 provides other technical benefits in terms of security and mobility in addition to the larger addressing space. Also, IPv6 design improves network performance and reduces routing time by having a fixed header size. The DiffServ mechanism performance is boosted by IPv6 design because it leverages the Flow Label field in the IPv6 header. The edge router reads the required field values from the same layer and header during the packet classification process and it does not need to go to the transport layer data. However, still, stream assignment to the class of service, and setting the preferences within the class is a manual setup and is a static operation. All those limitations are not suitable for the IoT system since the Internet of Things is placing new demands on network infrastructure due to the diverse application domains (e.g., smart health, smart city). Under different contexts and domains, IoT applications could adopt different classification methods and QoS policies compared with the current web applications. Moreover, the number of connected devices and the amount of generated data will become an increasing stress on the Internet network. Although there is an option for companies to pay a certain price to make their services reliable and to improve performance that user experienced, the Internet standard still enforces limitations and challenges such as number of QoS traffic classes, complexity, and cost of deployment, and lack of scalability.

Software Defined Networking (SDN) is a potential solution to the problems faced by traditional computer networks like the Internet. Unlike traditional networking system where the traffic control-plane and forwarding-plane are installed and tied together in one single element, SDN technology brings the capability to decouple the control-plane from data-plane to enhance the network evolution, interoperability, and scalability. It allows network owners and administrators to programmatically initialize, control, and manage network behavior by decoupling the control plane from the data-plane.

SDN improves the interoperability between multi-vendor products and removes vendor lock-in state which are common drawbacks in the traditional network. It decreases the overhead of network element configuration and troubleshooting, leading to the optimized capital and operational expenditures for IT enterprises. Additionally, software-driven networks enable the possibility of network control by a software application and make the network management more efficient, quick and flexible. Any network operator could develop customized solutions based on the business need and enforce it through a centralized controller. Beside the flexible and scalable QoS management, the network provider could leverage SDN technology to manage other aspects of the network like security and resource provisioning and configuration, and network monitoring in a more flexible and efficient way [6]–[9]. SDN technology could be deployed either in IPv4- or IPv6-based network, so both IPv6 and SDN could coexist in the network, each bringing different feature for network efficiency.

The main question addressed in this work is how resource allocation can be matched to the IoT application QoS needs while considering the resource capabilities and limitations. Therefore, the goal is to build an adaptive and flexible QoS model which could keep pace with dynamic business and application requirements. To do so, we propose a status-aware and SLA-aware routing mechanism across software-defined communication networks (internet or private network). Unlike similar works, we implement multi-path and load-balancing approaches in the model to enhance network throughput and system availability, along with user experience. It is worth noting that SLA is a formal negotiated agreement between service providers and customers and it can cover many aspects of their relationship such as the performance of services, customer care, billing, and provisioning.

In the classical network, there is no way to fetch the status information directly from the network elements in a centralized and real-time way, and consequently the network topology and the QoS parameters. Therefore, current routing path mechanisms do not consider the current network status e.g., packet loss, delay, or available bandwidth in the path calculation process. Besides, link cost metrics used in the routing mechanism are same for all the application type. But, our model assigns different path for the same data dynamically depending on the current network status and link cost metrics are diverse depending on the application type.

The rest of the paper is organized as follows. In Section II, we provide a review of related studies. In Section III, we present the routing model and provide the mathematical formulation of the problem. Section IV details the experiments and results. We then provide a detailed analysis of the results and finally conclude our work in Section V.

II. PREVIOUS WORKS

Internet of Things continues to evolve and expand in terms of domains, interconnected-devices, data, and applications, and as a result, IoT specifics challenges are getting more bigger and complex [10]. Both research communities and industrial enterprises are working on IoT-specific challenges to solve technological barriers which slow down the evolution of IoT. QoS management as one of the critical subsystem in IoT framework attracted the attentions in research institute. To provide QoS in the IoT, it is necessary to ensure suitable mechanisms at each layer of the IoT since various applications could have the dependency on the different QoS attributes, which must be provided by a specific IoT layer. Various research communities have attempted to define high-level QoS schemes taking into account the multi-layer IoT architecture, service components, enabling technologies, and data classification. Others are proposing solutions in the aspects of the resource identification, routing protocols, clustering, and topology update within any leveraged networking technologies in IoT system.

Wireless Sensor Networks (WSNs), widely used in IoT infrastructure, are comprised of hundreds or thousands of low-ends battery-powered devices. A large number of the studies investigate on resource management within such an constrained environment. Proposed solutions differ on the design methodology and details of the quality factors. Energy and bandwidth efficiency, storage and coverage optimization, or data accuracy enhancement are mostly targeted in those researches [11] [12]. For instance, in [13], the authors present the computational QoS model for WSN routing using the directed graph theory and considering the response time, reliability, and availability as QoS factors. Mostafaei [14] developed the Reliable Routing Distributed Learning Automaton (RRDLA) algorithm to streamline the performance of the wireless sensor network, and therefore reduce energy consumption within it, by means of the modeling and simulation. End-to-end delay, packet delivery rate, network lifetime, and the number of times are parameters modeled in RRDLA.

Middleware-based approach solution [15] is one of the promising approaches to manage QoS within heterogeneous IoT environment. Within proposed model by Heinzelman [15], applications sends QoS requirement to the middleware and then middleware configures networks devices to meet the application expectations. This approach enables the adaptation of the code allocation on the basis of the current application requirements. If application QoS requirements from application are not feasible to fulfill by network resources, middleware negotiates a new QoS guarantee with both application and network.

Other IoT enabling technologies like the Internet and the cellular access networks (e.g.3G, LTE) have the evolved QoS functions within their closed systems, although their integration into IoT bring issues and limitations. With the realization of the 5G technology, the barriers of the access networks are rectified, since 5G provides less-delay high-bandwidth access network for the IoT system. the continuous researches are ongoing to enhancement QoS within 5G network leveraging mostly learning-based techniques for to adapt system design with IoT use-cases [16]. The QoS magnification within Internet and computer network are involving new mechanisms like Diffserve, InterSev, and MPLS, and technologies like IPv6. As described in previous sections, The Internet still imposes complications in terms of QoS deployment in IoT space and since static QoS differentiation mechanism could not meet the requirements of dynamic and data-centric applications.

The idea of SDN presented new research topics in the literature, not only in computer networks, but also in other networking technology like cellular network and Wireless Sensor Network in more recent years and it is getting more promising vision by the appearance of IoT and also SDN success stories. It led to the widespread adoption of Software-Defined WSNs (SDWSNs)and Software Defined Wireless Network (SDWN) [17]–[19]. As a more recent field, research domain SD-IoT aims to integrate SDN into the IoT framework to improve the system control and management. For instance, the SD-IoT framework model in [6] offers as centralized control system over security services (SDSec), storage services (SDS) and infrastructure resources. Few studies [8] attempt to improve resource utilization in terms of data acquisition, transmission, and processing within the IoT framework. For instance, UbiFlow offered in [9] proposes an efficient flow control and mobility management framework in urban multi-network environment using distributed SDN controllers. In [20], the authors propose a traffic-aware quality-of-service routing scheme in Software-Defined Internet of Things network. They exploit features such as flow-based nature, and network flexibility, in order to fulfill QoS requirements of each flow in the network. The authors in [21] propose an application-aware QoS routing algorithm for SDN-based IoT networking to guarantee multiple QoS requirements of high-priority IoT applications and to adapt to the current network status for better routing paths. Although these efforts argue that software-defined technology can facilitate IoT system and resource management, most proposals target high-level architectural and framework enhancement and are more like conceptual and analytical models, and need to be implemented and assessed.

The concept of SD-IoT is in its infancy and standardization efforts in terms of framework, protocol and software-defined applications are still underway [22]. We realized a lack of study in the field of performance management in which heterogeneous devices, network resources, and application needs could be managed in an easy and flexible way. The currently designed solutions are very high-level and mainly focused on improving one or multiple QoS factors in a closed subsystem of IoT. Most works lack of flexibility and scalability considering IoT heterogeneity and dynamic natures in terms of applications and services.

We are working on an middleware-based QoS management framework for IoT application, to control and allocate IoT infrastructure resources within a multi-platform environment including transport and sensing network. Our model takes advantages of SDN characteristics to takes into account the application QoS preferences and network elements status to allocate resources effectively, guaranteeing application productivity and maximizing network performance.

As part of the end to end framework, in the next section, we propose a routing algorithm to determine the best possible path for IoT applications' traffic across the software-driven network. The proposed algorithm is presented in a mathematical model for the route optimization problem between two connected things. The model would be developed as an customized application on top of the SDN controller, and it takes advantage of the SDN technology to consider the network resource status in the route calculation process.

III. ROUTING MODEL

SDN architecture [23] is made of three logical layers. The data plane layer is composed of physical devices that forwards traffic packets, The control plane includes the centralized networking controller, supervises all network traffic and makes decisions about where the traffic must be forwarded. The application layer represents the services that interact with the controller to specify the networking needs of the applications in terms of security, configuration, and management. The communication between the forwarding devices and controller is done through Southbound interfaces. A controller exercises direct control over the states of the data-plane devices via well-defined Application Programming Interfaces (APIs). OpenFlow [24] is the first standard Southbound interface. On the other hand, the Northbound interfaces enable the programmable network functions that tell the controller how to manage the network. Thus, the value of the Northbound interfaces is tied to the innovative and adaptive network services aligned with business and users needs. The customized network services are softwares and could be implemented as plug-ins to the centralized controller or any other standalone environment interacting with the controller through APIs. Supporting APIs in SDN hide the complexity and heterogeneity of the physical infrastructure. East/westbound interfaces are a special case of interfaces required by distributed controllers. They are used to interconnect the SDN architecture with external SDN-based network architectures or legacy networks.

In this work, we assume that SDN technology has been integrated into IoT framework, so that underlying network resources are SDN-enabled and the SDN controller resides in the IoT middleware layer. This schema would take advantages of northbound interfaces to design a centralized routing algorithm to manage IoT specific application needs and accordingly infrastructure resources including network elements and IoT gateways as interface toward low-end sensing devices. The quality of performance metrics taken into account are packet loss rate, delay, and bandwidth as they represent the main QoS metrics.

The proposed routing model is based on the well-known Network Design Problems (NDPs): Multi-Commodity Flow Problem (MCFP) and Constrained-Based Routing (CBR). The term multi-commodity (opposed to a single-commodity) is related to the fact that multiple demands could simultaneously arrive in the system and ask for routing resources in the network, which is very common in the communication and computer networks, as well as in IoT systems. The objective of the MCFP problem is to flow the different traffic demands from various sources to the distinct destinations through the network at minimum cost without exceeding the network link capacities.

Constraint-based routing denotes a class of routing algorithms where path selection decisions are made based on a set of requirements or constraints, in addition to the destination. These constraints can be imposed either by administrative policies or QoS requirements. We consider the network QoS status as well as application QoS constraints in our formulation. The objective is a minimum-cost feasible solution for the constraint-based routing problem to find the cheapest possible way of sending a certain amount of flow through the network. The decision making framework and QoS routing algorithm are illustrated in Figure 1 and Algorithm 1, respectively. Operation mode of algorithm and element details are provided as we describe the mathematical model.

We suppose a network of interconnected nodes where each link has a dedicated capacity. We also assume that all network nodes are OpenFlow-enabled and connected to one centralized SDN controller [25]. The SDN-based network can be represented by a strongly connected graph G = (V,E) where V = {1, 2, ..., v} denotes the set of nodes (OpenFlow-enabled network elements) and E =$\{(i, j) : i, j \in V, i \neq j\}$ denotes the set of edges, also referred to the bi-directional links between OpenFlow network elements. Each link (i, j) has the associated maximum bandwidth B_{ij}, available bandwidth b_{ij}, delay d_{ij}, and packet loss ratio pl_{ij}. In our context, the delay represents the total link delay consisting of processing, propagation, transmission, and queueing delay. *Network Topology and Link Status* refers to those parameters, and could be stored in centralized database, called *Topology Database*.

On the other hand, K = {1, 2, ..., k} and $\mid K \mid= k$, represent the set of different commodities, also determined as *IoT application demands* in decision-making framework, to be routed on the network graph. For each demand $k \in K$, three parameters are given: S^k as the source of the demand, T^k as the destination of the demand, and F^k as the positive demand volume. Demand volume represents either the traffic volume or the required bandwidth between a pair of nodes and the unit of the demand volume needs to be consistent with the unit of link capacities. *SLA-based Application QoS Database* elements refer to D^k_{SLA}, PL^k_{SLA}, and B^k_{SLA} representing the acceptable values of delay, packet loss ratio, and average required bandwidth respectively, which are agreed in the application-service provider SLA for IoT service *k*. The parameters $S^k, T^k, F^k, D^k_{SLA}, PL^k_{SLA}$, and B^k_{SLA} are considered as the input to the routing path calculation algorithm. The algorithm takes the information about each demand as well as the network link information (b_{ij}, d_{ij}, and pl_{ij}) and calculates the best possible path p^k for each new-arrival demand *k* between the source and destination across the SDN network with minimum cost flow. Network topology and link status information are regularly gathered and updated by the SDN controller. According to the OpenFlow specification v1.0, Topology Discovery function as the defacto standard function is implemented in all controllers. This function enables the controller to discover a network topology of the entire SDN infrastructure. To calculate Link QoS status, we can take advantage of the implemented counters in the OpenFlow-enabled network element. Those counters are stored packet processing/statistical records in particular tables in flow pr port basis. The system could provide multiple paths for any demand *k* aiming not to violate the accepted QoS level by any demands. All determined paths for service *k* are from source S^k to destination T^k so that each one routes a portion of the whole demand volume F^k. We assume that there exists no pair of flows with the same origin and destination.

Objective function: The objective is to route application flows in the network with minimum cost in respect to the particular cost metrics for each application. Equation (1) represents the objective function where C_{ij} is the unit cost of link (i, j) and X^k_{ij} as a variable represents the amount of volume corresponding to the demand *k* to be routed on the link (i, j).

$$Minimize \sum_{(i,j)\in E} \sum_{k} C_{ij} X^k_{ij} \tag{1}$$

The link cost metric in our model is represented as a weighted sum of the available link bandwidth, packet loss ratio, and delay, as per (2), where C_{ij} expresses the cost of link (i, j), metrics b_{ij}, pl_{ij} , and d_{ij} refer to the available link bandwidth, packet loss ratio, and delay in link (i, j), respectively; all dynamically calculated based on the current network status monitored by the controller.

$$C_{ij} = \alpha \times b_{ij} + \beta \times pl_{ij} + \gamma \times d_{ij} \tag{2}$$

The coefficient α, β, and γ as scaling factors have the relation expressed in (3). So, each metric can have different weight to give a priority to a particular one. Regarding our application classification based on traffic sensitivity to the delay and bandwidth, we could define a diverse weight for each metric in each particular application class. *Application classifier* within decision-making framework could provide dynamic input to differentiate application classes and enforce the result in traffic prioritization and Queuing mechanisms.

$$\alpha + \beta + \gamma = 1, 0 \leq \alpha, \beta, \gamma \leq 1 \tag{3}$$

Among the quality-related metrics used for link cost formulation, bandwidth is positive so that the higher value means the higher service quality. Delay and packet loss ratio are negative, meaning that the higher the value, the lower the service quality. Additionally, each metric has a different unit. Delay unit is in *seconds*, the bandwidth unit is *bps*, and loss ratio is a digit represented in *percentage*. To express a weighted sum of independent metrics, values of those metrics need to be adjusted theoretically to a common scale. We use the feature scaling method [26] to normalize the range of those independent metrics. This method re-scales the range of all values and brings them all into the range [0, 1]. Equations (4) to (6) present the normalization formulas for each metric. To set a boundary for each variable, maximum and minimum ranges could either have a constant value or adjust dynamically based on the network topology information at any given time.

$$b'_{ij} = \frac{b_{max} - b_{ij}}{b_{max} - b_{min}}, b_{min} \leq b_{ij} \leq b_{max} \tag{4}$$

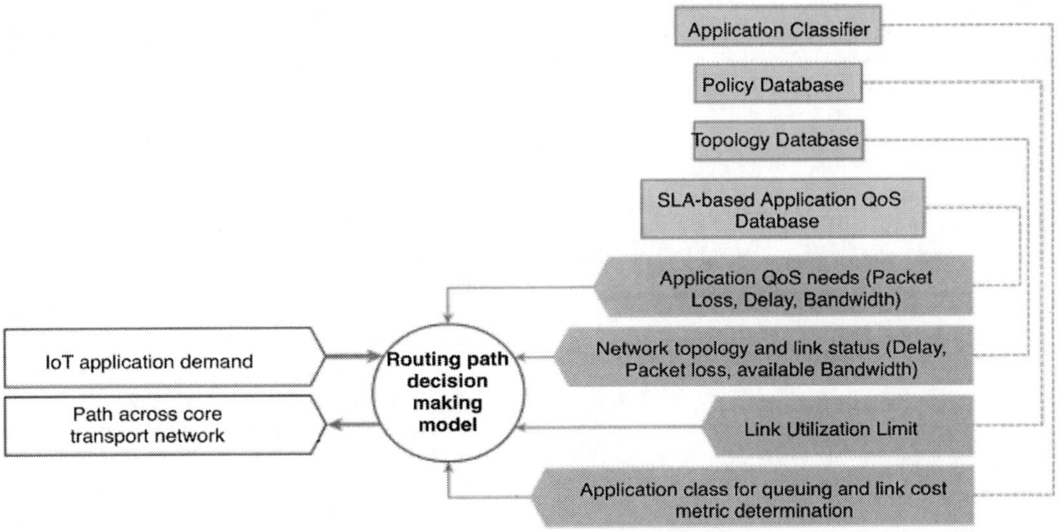

Figure 1. Routing path decision making framework - Parameters (gray boxes) and components (orange boxes) which define the input parameters.

Input: $G = (V, E)$ as network topology: $V = \{1, 2, ..., v\}$ as nodes and $E = \{(i, j) : i, j \in V, i \neq j\}$ as bidirectional links
Input: (S^k,T^k, F^k) per each demand k in K: $S^k \in V$ as Source of demand, $T^k \in V$ as Destination of demand k, $F^k \geq 0$ as Total demand volume, $[Mbps]$
Output: P^k: Routing path across network for demand k
for (i, j) in E **do**
Get network link QoS parameters ($b_{ij} \geq 0$, $pl_{ij} \geq 0$, $d_{ij} \geq 0$, $B_{ij} > 0$;
Calculate the current link utilization rate ;
Get the link utilization limit $u_{Threshold}$;
if Link utilization rate $\geq u_{Threshold}$ **then** ;
Exclude this link from the logical network topology to calculate paths for current active demands ;
end;
end ;
for k in K **do**
Get Max acceptable delay D^k_{SLA}, Max acceptable packet loss PL^k_{SLA}, and Min required bandwidth B^k_{SLA} for each demand k in K from SLA-DB ;
Set the link cost metrics depending on the application class, if any ;
end;
for k in K **do**
Calculate the best-fit path per each demand k in K based on the proposed mathematical model;
end;

Figure 2. Proposed QoS support routing algorithm

$$pl'_{ij} = \frac{pl_{ij} - pl_{min}}{pl_{max} - pl_{min}}, pl_{min} \leq pl_{ij} \leq pl_{max} \quad (5)$$

$$d'_{ij} = \frac{d_{ij} - d_{min}}{d_{max} - d_{min}}, d_{min} \leq d_{ij} \leq d_{max} \quad (6)$$

Constraint function: we introduce the several types of conditions which are imposed by the network and application.

• Path delay constraint for each demand is defined in (7), where d^k_p is the end-to-end delay for the routing path p^k determined for demand k, and D^k_{SLA} is the maximum acceptable delay for demand k agreed in SLA.

$$d^k_p \leq D^k_{SLA} \quad (7)$$

Delay metric is an additive metric. So, total delay p_p in the path p from one source to a destination is calculated by the summing of the delay on each link (i, j) across the path, formulated in (8).

$$d_p = \sum_{(i,j) \in p} d_{ij} \quad (8)$$

So, (7) can be replaced by Equation (9):

$$\sum_{(i,j) \in E, P^k} d_{ij} \leq D^k_{SLA}, \forall k \in K \quad (9)$$

• Constraint for path packet loss ratio in each demand is defined in (10), where pl^k_p is the total packet loss ratio for the routing path p^k determined for demand k and PL^k_{SLA} is the maximum acceptable packet loss ratio for demand k agreed in SLA.

$$pl^k_p \leq PL^k_{SLA} \quad (10)$$

Packet loss is a multiplicative metrics. Packet loss ratio along the path is determined in (11), where pl_p refers to the packet loss ratio for path p and pl_{ij} refers to the packet loss ratio for a particular link (i, j) across the path p:

$$pl_p = 1 - \prod_{(i,j)\in p} (1 - pl_{ij}) \tag{11}$$

If the packet loss ratio in the network link is very small and close to zero, packet loss measure could be considered as an additive measure and can be approximately simplified by (12).

$$pl_p = \sum_{(i,j)\in p} pl_{ij} \tag{12}$$

So, (10) can be expressed by (13):

$$\sum_{(i,j)\in E, P^k} pl_{ij} \leq PL^k_{SLA}, \forall k \in K \tag{13}$$

• Link capacity constraint is formulated in (14). In multi-commodity environment, each link could be part of multiple routing paths used by different commodities. Then, the summation of the volume of the different commodity in any link (i, j) must be less than the available link bandwidth b_{ij}, which is measurable in the SDN transport network. This constraint could fulfill the context of the congestion management in the network.

$$\sum_{k\in K} X^k_{ij} \leq b_{ij}, \forall (i,j) \in E \tag{14}$$

• Link utilization/load balancing constraint. To choose the optimized and well-fit path for a given traffic, we consider the link utilization constraint in the path allocation process. Since link bandwidth as one of link status information is monitored and stored by controller in network topology database, link utilization rate on any given link (i, j) can be measured by dividing the current link bandwidth with maximum link capacity, expressed in (15) in a unit of percentage.

$$Utilization\ Ratio\ (i,j) = \frac{B_{ij} - b_{ij}}{B_{ij}} \tag{15}$$

Generally, the link with utilization rate 70% 80% is susceptible to congestion [27]. To balance traffic across links and to avoid congestion, we define a limit for the link utilization rate so that the proposed routing algorithm excludes links with link utilization rate higher than this limit from the path calculation scenario. The link utilization limit can be provided in a policy database accessed by the controller. This limit can be defined either as a constant value given by network providers or as a dynamically adjustable value. In the later approach, the controller applies a developed logic considering the traffic volume, demand arrival rate, and network status at any given time. We formulate the load balancing constraint with (16), where $\cup_{Threshold}$ is the link utilization limit:

$$\sum_{k\in K} X^k_{ij} \leq b_{ij} + (\cup_{Threshold} - 1) * B_{ij}, \forall (i,j) \in E \tag{16}$$

Regarding the delay/bandwidth threshold, unlike IT applications which are categorized based on the type of traffic, IoT application could be classified from different perspectives such as the type of information they manage, the type of recipient (person or system oriented), and the criticality level of services they provide. Currently, IoT systems still suffer from the lack of standardized mechanisms to represent the diverse application requirements, also as reference for our proposed model. To setup the reasonable thresholds for QoS metrics, we plan to do experiments with multiple applications within end to end deployed framework, also to gather data from production applications, and to calculate the average value for those metrics.

• The flow conservation law is formulated with (17). It states that the total incoming flow into each node in the network equals the total outgoing flow from that node, except for the source and destination nodes of flow. It also guarantees the same bandwidth in all links across the determined path for a particular demand.

$$\sum_{(i,j)\in E} X^k_{ij} - \sum_{(j,i)\in E} X^k_{ji} = \begin{cases} F^k, i = S^k \\ -F^k, i = T^k \\ 0, i \neq S^k \& T^k \end{cases} \tag{17}$$

In the offered mathematical formulation, the number of variables is $|E||K|$ and the number of constraints is $|E||K| + |K| + |E|$. Since the number of the QoS parameters used in our model is more than one, it is proven to be $N\rho$-complete [28] as the complex problem. The complexity of standard Dijkstra algorithm is O(v^2), and with more efficient implementation in link-state protocols like Open Shortest Path First (OSPF) will be O($vlogv$).

Compared with OSPF in which computational requirements of calculating link state information rise rapidly exponentially/logarithmically as the size and complexity of the network increase, the complexity of our proposed algorithm is driven by the multiplication of number of links and nodes. Theoretically, it can be concluded that the proposed algorithm could provide less convergence time as could be the most-fitted solution for mission-critical IoT applications. However practical analysis would be needed to provide more insight about the improvement level.

IV. Experiments and Results

To investigate the feasibility and the performance of the proposed model, we implemented it in A Mathematical Programming Language (*AMPL*). According to our mathematical formulation, the number of variables is $|E|$ $|K|$ and the number of constraints is $|E|$ $|K|$ + $|K|$+$|E|$. This problem is $N\rho - complete$ due to the number of QoS parameters [61]. Since the objective function and all constraints are in the linear format and only the values of the variable X could be discrete, this model is classified as Mixed Integer Programming (MIP) problem. Thus, we paired *AMPL* with the *CPLEX* solver to solve the problem. *CPLEX* uses branch-and-bound algorithm to find the optimal solution for Mixed Integer Programming problem.

Bellman-Ford and *Dijkstra* are the two main algorithms used in a weighted graph to compute the shortest paths from a single source to a destination. In the current packet switching network, Bellman-Ford algorithm has enabled the development of distance-vector routing protocols while the Dijkstra algorithm introduces link state routing protocols. In both, each router learns about remote networks from the neighbor routers or the configuration to build the routing table. Link state routing protocols enable a router to build and track a full map of all network links while distance vector protocols work with less information about the network area. Since our routing model is contextually similar to link-state protocols, we aim to evaluate the performance of the proposed routing model with the Open Shortest-Path First (OSPF), which is one of the well-established and widely-adopted link-state routing protocols. OSPF considers link bandwidth as the link cost metric to calculate the routing. The link cost calculation formula in OSPF is determined by (19):

$$Interface\ cost = \frac{Reference\ bandwidth}{Interface\ bandwidth} \quad (18)$$

In Cisco products, the default reference bandwidth value in OSPF is 100 Mbps (108bps). Hence, we have the following equation as the cost of link (i, j):

$$Cost_{ij} = \frac{100}{B_{ij}} \quad (19)$$

The QoS requirements of IoT applications are not clearly defined because of the data-oriented and diverse needs. To facilitate the implementation of our experiment environment, we map the IoT application classes onto the IoT data delivery model as in Table II and we assign dynamic cost metrics for the different application classes of Table I.

In Table I, we present three different queues in each port of the OpenFlow-enabled network elements: (1) Priority Queue (PQ) as the most prioritized queue includes mission-critical applications with intensive delay sensitivity. If the delay requirement of application is less than a pre-defined threshold, it is marked as a high-prioritized demand and it is inserted in PQ of egress ports of network elements. (2) Q1 represents the data-centric application with bandwidth sensitivity, and less delay-sensitive compared to the pre-defined threshold. (3) Q2 contains applications with no strict QoS requirements, also called the best-effort application.

For the delay-sensitive application, we set both packet loss and delay as the metrics and for the bandwidth-sensitive application, packet loss and bandwidth are considered as link cost metrics. For the Best Effort (BE) application, either the combination of packet loss, delay, and bandwidth would be used in our routing model or the traditional less-complex best-effort routing algorithm could be applied.

In the experiment, we characterize the application from different classes (delay-centric and BW-centric) with different quality requirements for each network performance metric and we calculate delay, packet loss, and link utilization rate of the paths determined by our model. The results are compared with the characteristics of the calculated paths by OSPF routing model. The experiment scenario is visualized in Figure 3.

Multiple network topologies (Topology A, B, C, and D-elaborated in Tables III, IV, V, and VI, respectively) designed to run the test ensure the path diversity between any pair of nodes. We define the network topology and assign the

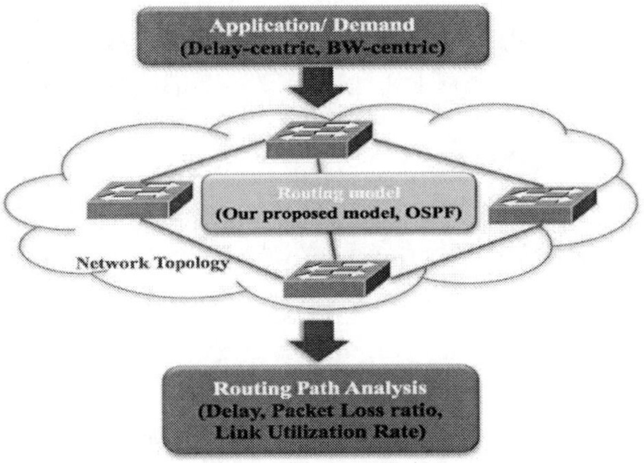

Figure 3. Experiment and performance analysis scenario.

maximum capacity, available bandwidth, delay, and packet loss ratio for network links. Also, we present the service demands specifying the source, destination, and volume as well as the QoS requirements in terms of delay, packet loss, and minimum bandwidth. The simulated demands are directed towards the bottlenecks to investigate delay and throughput of the Delay-centric and Bandwidth-centric traffic, respectively. Both single-commodity and multi-commodity scenarios are investigated under the same network situation. In the single demand scenario, we define an individual demand, while in the multi-demand scenario, we create more stress on the network by defining multiple simultaneous demands.

1) Result analysis - Delay: The path delay and packet loss ratio for all delay-centric demands characterized in the different topologies are demonstrated in Table VII and Table VIII for single-commodity and multi-demand scenario, respectively. Referring to the results, we observe that our model finds the optimized routing paths in terms of the delay and packet loss for the delay-centric demand compared to the OSPF. Our model can enhance the performance and efficiency of delay-centric applications. Event-driven IoT applications in smart cities are often mission-critical and delay intolerant, such as the emergency signals and safety related applications. To be effective, the information should be transmitted in a limited time frame.

On the other hand, BW-centric demands are not concerned about the delay and our model looks for the links with the optimized high available bandwidth and lower packet loss rate. The results depicted in Tables IX and X show the delay associated with the paths calculated by our model. It is almost lower than the delay associated with the paths calculated by OSPF for BW-centric applications, in both single and multi-commodity environment. Since we set the delay constraint in our mathematical model for all application classes, our model aims to find the best-fit path with the acceptable level of delay for BW-centric application depending on the network status at any given time.

SDN-based middleware in the networking layer makes our model dynamically aware of the network status and have access to the SLA-related application QoS databases. Besides,

TABLE I. APPLICATION CLASSIFICATION AND QUEUEING POLICY IN OPENFLOW NETWORK ELEMENT: D^k_{max} AS MAXIMUM ACCEPTABLE DELAY FOR SERVICE k, BWk_{min} AS THE MINIMUM REQUIRED BW FOR SERVICE k, $D_{Threshold}$ AS THE DELAY THRESHOLD, $BW_{Threshold}$ AS THE BW THRESHOLD

Application Class	QoS attributes	Priority	Type of queue	Traffic Class mapped with Cisco classification
Delay-Centric (Mission Critical)	$D^k_{max} \leq D_{Threshold}$	1	PQ (Priority Queue)	EF (Expedited Forwarding)
Bandwidth-Centric (Multimedia application)	$D^k_{max} \geq D_{Threshold}$, $BW^k_{min} \geq BW_{Threshold}$	2	Q1	AF (Assured Forwarding)
General (Non-Real time analytic application)	No strict QoS needs	3	Q2	BE (Best Effort)

TABLE II. MAPPING IoT APPLICATION CLASSIFICATION AND LINK COST METRICS

IoT Application	Application class	Link cost metric
Mission-critical, Event-related application	Delay-centric	Delay and Packet-loss rate
Continuous application (Query-driven, Real-time monitoring)	Bandwidth-centric	Bandwidth and Packet-loss rate
General application (Non-real time monitoring)	BE	All three metrics

TABLE III. TOPOLOGY-A LINK CONFIGURATION

Link	Max BW(Mbps)	PacketLoss	Delay(ms)	Available BW(Mbps)	Link	Max BW(Mbps)	PacketLoss(%)	Delay(ms)	Available BW(Mbps)
(1,2)	300	1%	0.01	300	(2,6)	400	2%	0.01	200
(1,4)	400	1%	0.02	400	(3,6)	600	2%	0.05	400
(1,5)	200	2%	0.01	200	(4,5)	400	1%	0.01	300
(2,3)	600	2%	0.02	300	(5,6)	300	1%	0.01	300
(2,5)	600	2%	0.05	200					

TABLE IV. TOPOLOGY-B LINK CONFIGURATION

Link	Max BW(Mbps)	PacketLoss(%)	Delay(ms)	Available BW(Mbps)	Link	Max BW(Mbps)	PacketLoss(%)	Delay(ms)	Available BW(Mbps)
(1,2)	400	1	0.01	200	(4,7)	600	1	0.01	200
(1,4)	600	2	0.02	300	(5,6)	400	1	0.01	300
(2,3)	300	1	0.02	300	(5,7)	300	1	0.01	200
(2,3)	200	2	0.01	150	(5,8)	200	2	0.02	100
(2,5)	300	1	0.02	300	(6,8)	300	1	0.01	200
(3,5)	400	1	0.05	200	(6,9)	300	2	0.02	1500
(3,6)	600	2	0.03	400	(7,8)	400	2	0.03	400
(4,5)	200	2	0.01	100	(8,9)	600	2	0.02	400

TABLE V. TOPOLOGY-C LINK CONFIGURATION

Link	Link BW (Mbps)	Packet loss(%)	Delay(ms)	Available BW(Mbps)	Link	Link BW(Mbps)	Packet loss(%)	Delay(ms)	Available BW(Mbps)
(1 2)	500	1	0.01	300	(5 6)	600	1.5	0.01	400
(1 4)	600	2	0.02	300	(5 12)	300	0	0.01	300
(1 5)	200	1.5	0.05	100	(6 10)	500	1.5	0.05	300
(2 3)	600	1.5	0.02	300	(7 8)	600	1.5	0.02	150
(2 5)	300	1.5	0.05	150	(7 10)	400	2	0.05	200
(2 6)	400	1.5	0.01	200	(8 9)	400	1.5	0.01	200
(2 9)	400	0	0.01	200	(8 11)	600	1.5	0.01	300
(3 6)	600	1.5	0.05	500	(10 11)	400	1.5	0.01	200
(3 7)	600	2	0.05	500	(11 12)	300	1	0.02	200
(4 5)	400	0	0.01	300					

this information is directly applied to the resource allocation process. Application sensitivity to delay or bandwidth leads to having different link cost metrics. For the mission-critical application, it seeks for the delay-less and loss-less paths, while meeting the capacity constraints, and the outcome is the least cost (least-delay) and SLA-respected paths. Also, the framework structure allocate dynamic paths regarding the current network link conditions, in case of any change in the network link status, the model will be notified and new QoS-respected paths are calculated for the flows based on

TABLE VI. TOPOLOGY-D LINK CONFIGURATION

Link	Link BW (Mbps)	Packet loss(%)	Delay(ms)	Available BW(Mbps)	Link	Link BW(Mbps)	Packet loss(%)	Delay(ms)	Available BW(Mbps)
(1 2)	400	1	0.01	200	(7 10)	600	1	0.01	400
(1 4)	600	2	0.02	300	(8 9)	300	2	0.02	200
(2 3)	300	1	0.02	300	(8 10)	200	1	0.01	200
(2 4)	200	2	0.01	150	(8 11)	300	2	0.01	100
(2 5)	300	1	0.02	300	(9 11)	400	1	0.01	200
(3 5)	400	1	0.05	200	(9 12)	600	2	0.02	400
(3 6)	600	2	0.01	400	(10 11)	600	1	0.01	400
(4 5)	600	2	0.03	400	(10 13)	300	2	0.02	250
(4 7)	200	1	0.01	100	(11 12)	200	1	0.01	100
(5 6)	600	2	0.01	400	(11 13)	200	2	0.02	200
(5 7)	300	1	0.01	200	(11 14)	300	1	0.01	200
(5 8)	200	2	0.02	100	(12 14)	200	2	0.02	100
(6 8)	300	1	0.01	200	(12 15)	600	1	0.01	200
(6 9)	600	2	0.02	400	(13 14)	300	2	0.01	200
(7 8)	400	2	0.02	400	(13 15)	300	2	0.02	100

TABLE VII. DELAY AND PACKET LOSS RATE: DELAY-CENTRIC APPLICATION IN SINGLE-DEMAND SCENARIO

		Single-Demand			
		Our model		OSPF	
		Delay (ms)	Loss rate (%)	Delay (ms)	Loss rate (%)
Topology-A	Delay-centric 1	0.06	3	0.07	4
	Delay-centric 2	0.03	2	0.06	3
	Delay-centric 3	0.05	4	0.08	5
Topology-B	Delay-centric 1	0.04	5	0.06	5
	Delay-centric 2	0.02	2	0.04	3
	Delay-centric 2	0.06	5	0.08	7
Topology-C	Delay-centric 1	0.03	2	0.1	6
	Delay-centric 2	0.05	4	0.11	4
	Delay-centric 3	0.03	1	0.07	3
	Delay-centric 4	0.03	3	0.08	5

TABLE VIII. DELAY AND PACKET LOSS RATE: DELAY-CENTRIC APPLICATION IN MULTI-DEMAND SCENARIO

			Multiple-Demand			
			Our model		OSPF	
			Delay (ms)	Loss rate (%)	Delay (ms)	Loss rate (%)
Topology A	Test1	Delay-centric 1	0.03	2	0.06	3
	Test2	Delay-centric 1	0.03	2	0.06	3
		Delay-centric 2	0.05	4	0.08	5
	Test3	Delay-centric 1	0.03	2	0.06	3
Topology B	Test 1	Delay-centric 1	0.04	5	0.06	6
		Delay-centric 1	0.03	2	0.05	3
	Test2	Delay-centric 1	0.04	5	0.06	6
		Delay-centric 2	0.03	2	0.05	3
	Test3	Delay-centric 1	0.04	5	0.06	6
		Delay-centric 2	0.03	2	0.05	3
Topology D	Test1	Delay-centric 1	0.04	4	0.08	8
		Delay-centric 2	0.04	4	0.06	6
	Test2	Delay-centric 1	0.04	4	0.08	8
		Delay-centric 2	0.04	4	0.06	6
		Delay-centric 3	0.02	2	0.04	4
	Test3	Delay-centric 1	0.04	4	0.08	8
		Delay-centric 2	0.04	4	0.07	7
		Delay-centric 3	0.02	2	0.04	4

new network situation. Thus, we can state that the application effectiveness and also customer satisfaction are reinforced in the offered QoS routing. In OSPF, the routing approach is to forward the demand through the links with the highest maximum capacity. The high-bandwidth links could not be always considered as the less-delay links since link delay is affected by other factors such as queueing and congestion.

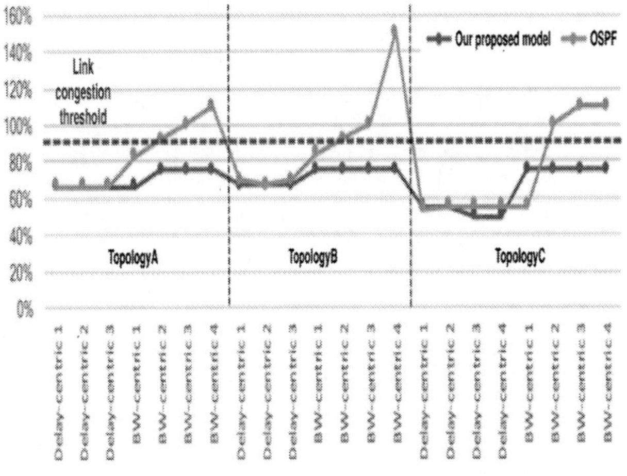

Figure 4. Maximum link utilization across network links in single-demand scenario.

TABLE IX. DELAY AND PACKET LOSS RATE: BANDWIDTH-CENTRIC APPLICATION IN SINGLE-DEMAND SCENARIO

		Single-Demand			
		Our model		OSPF	
		Delay	Packet lost rate(%)	Delay	Packet loss rate(%)
Topology A	BW-centric1	0.05	4	0.08	5
	BW-centric2	0.5	4	0.08	5
	BW-centric3	0.07	4	0.08	5
	BW-centric4	0.07	4	0.08	5
Topology B	BW-centric1	0.04	3	0.06	4
	BW-centric2	0.06	3	0.07	3
	BW-centric3	0.06	3.5	0.07	3
	BW-centric4	0.06	3.5	0.06	6
Topology C	BW-centric1	0.06	3	0.06	3
	BW-centric2	0.03	2.5	0.1	6
	BW-centric3	0.08	2.8	0.1	6
	BW-centric4	0.08	3.5	0.1	6

2) *Result analysis - throughput:* To assess the network throughput in our model, we measure the maximum link utilization rate across the network after allocating the paths for the demands. Figures 4 and 5 demonstrate the maximum link utilization rate in all experiments for single and multi-demand scenarios, respectively.

TABLE X. DELAY AND PACKET LOSS RATE: BANDWIDTH-CENTRIC APPLICATION IN MULTI-DEMAND SCENARIO

			Multiple-Demand			
			Our model		OSPF	
			Delay (ms)	Loss rate (%)	Delay (ms)	Loss rate (%)
Topology A	Test1	BW-centric1	0.05	4	0.08	5
	Test2	BW-centric1	0.05	4	0.08	5
		BW-centric2	0.06	3	0.07	4
	Test3	BW-centric1	0.06	3	0.07	4
Topology B	Test 1	BW-centric1	0.03	3	0.07	4
	Test2	BW-centric1	0.03	3	0.07	4
		BW-centric2	0.07	6	0.08	8
	Test3	BW-centric1	0.03	3	0.07	4
		BW-centric2	0.07	6	0.08	8
		BW-centric3	0.02	2	0.02	2
Topology D	Test1	BW-centric1	0.06	5	0.07	7
	Test2	BW-centric1	0.06	5	0.07	7
		BW-centric2	0.08	4	0.08	8
	Test3	BW-centric1	0.06	5	0.07	7
		BW-centric2	0.08	4	0.08	8
		BW-centric3	0.04	5	0.02	3

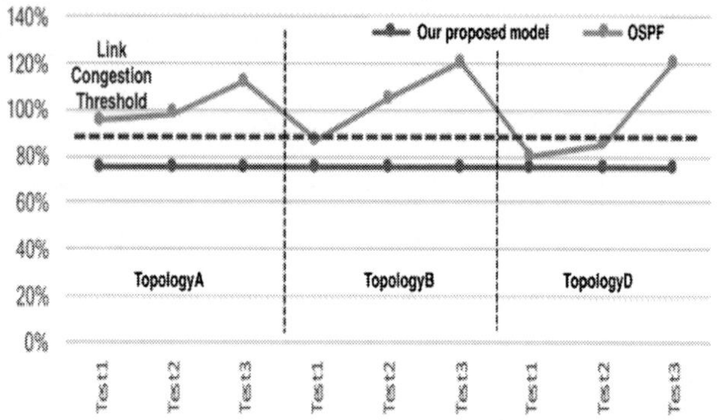

Figure 5. Maximum link utilization across network links in multi-demand scenario.

For the link utilization limit in our load balancing constraint, we set the predefined limit as 75%. Therefore, in the graphs, it can be seen that our model keeps the link utilization rate stable with the maximum 75% while respecting to the other constraints. On the contrary, we could see that the maximum link utilization rate across the network with the same configuration exceeds 100% when running the OSPF routing protocol. When link utilization exceeds 100% in theory (and about 85% in practice), the link is considered congested. Consequently, the demands passing through the congested link could not be served as desired and they may suffer from more delay and loss. Obviously, the rate of the congestion is increased in the multi-commodity environment with the arrival of more bandwidth-intensive demands. The congestion costs a lot for the delay sensitive applications and they might not fulfill their missions depending on the extent they are impacted and delayed. Besides, our model is aware of the current link utilization rate and it excludes the links with the load more than the predefined limit from the path calculation process. This can be considered a congestion prevention method so that the links with the highest available bandwidth and less utilization rate are discovered by our model to avoid the congestion and balance the load across the network links. Our model could be designed in the way to apply different link utilization limits depending on the network status and demand arrival rate to meet application QoS needs.

In our model, when multiple BW-intensive demand requests for data transfer service, the multipath approach is applied if one path could not provide the requested bandwidth. The BW-intensive applications are delay-tolerant compared to the delay-centric applications. Since the proposed model is aware of the currently available link bandwidth, it seeks to direct the flow toward the links with the higher available bandwidth which cost less.

Differently, OSPF does not have access to the currently available bandwidth and the utilization rate. It directs the demand flows toward the high capacity links and the same path could be assigned for a particular demand, independent of the current network status. So, it could cause congestion and failure in the high-load links. Consequently, the demand performance through the failed links are impacted in terms of the delay and loss. The effectiveness of the delay-sensitive demands passing through the congested link might be degraded by undesired delay, or even the transferred data could be useless because of its late arrival. To make it clear, we demonstrate the details of the paths calculated for experiment Test3-Topology B in which we characterize multiple demands (two delay-centric and three BW-centric) arriving the network. It can be seen that we have congestion in two links (4-7) and (5-7) which transfer data for four demands. Two of them are delay-centric demands and they could be impacted by the link congestion. Noting that to have the multi-path approach in OSPF networks, we need to implement load-balancers across the network. Also, to avoid the congestion across the OSPF-based network, the QoS mechanisms such as queueing and congestion control methods should be implemented in all the network elements. Though the queueing and priority scheduling policies could impact the behavior of the system in order to determine what demands to be removed in the congestion situation, the active demands and the network situation have the major impacts on the consequences. In general, the implementation of QoS mechanisms across a large network is resource-intensive, time intensive, and a complex task. It is error-prone because of the technical resource involvement. Moreover, in OSPF, the speed of convergence and the system adaptability to application needs and network changes are low.

V. CONCLUSION

The large number of IoT devices enable a wide variety of services in many different application domains such as smart city, smart transport, smart home, and smart health. There must be QoS approaches at every layer of the IoT architecture to ensure an acceptable level of performance especially for safety applications.

The main contribution of this work is the proposition of a flexible and programmable control layer to provide customized QoS support services for IoT applications. It is achieved by the integration of SDN technology into IoT system architecture. This scheme overcomes the challenge of the dynamic and diverse definition of the SLA and application QoS in the IoT. We proposed a status-aware and SLA-aware routing mechanism across the core transport software-defined network. SDN technology enables, in one hand, the possibility of real time monitoring of network statistical information and calculating network status, and in the other hand, to get application requirements dynamically to determine the best-fit routing path for the data transmission. Multi-path and load-balancing approaches implemented in the model lead to enhancing the network throughput and increasing system availability, which is crucial for mission-critical applications. All those features in addition to the capability of enforcing different cost metrics for different application types, our model seeks to find the less-delay and less-loss rate paths not only for delay-centric applications but also for bandwidth-centric applications. From the scalability and flexibility aspects, the system could be evolved interfacing with different routing algorithms to be applied to different application types in different network situations.

REFERENCES

[1] T. Kurakova, "Overview of the internet of things," *Proceedings of the Internet of things and its enablers (INTHITEN)*, pp. 82–94, 2013.

[2] F. Y. Okay and S. Ozdemir, "Routing in fog-enabled iot platforms: A survey and an sdn-based solution," *IEEE Internet of Things Journal*, vol. 5, no. 6, pp. 4871–4889, 2018.

[3] A. Zanella, N. Bui, A. Castellani, L. Vangelista, and M. Zorzi, "Internet of things for smart cities," *IEEE Internet of Things journal*, vol. 1, no. 1, pp. 22–32, 2014.

[4] R. Braden, D. Clark, and S. Shenker, "Rfc1633: Integrated services in the internet architecture: an overview," pp. 1–33, 1994.

[5] S. Blake *et al.*, "An architecture for differentiated services," Tech. Rep., 1998.

[6] Y. Jararweh *et al.*, "Sdiot: a software defined based internet of things framework," *Journal of Ambient Intelligence and Humanized Computing*, vol. 6, no. 4, pp. 453–461, 2015.

[7] J. Liu, Y. Li, M. Chen, W. Dong, and D. Jin, "Software-defined internet of things for smart urban sensing," *IEEE communications magazine*, vol. 53, no. 9, pp. 55–63, 2015.

[8] N. Bizanis and F. A. Kuipers, "Sdn and virtualization solutions for the internet of things: A survey," *IEEE Access*, vol. 4, pp. 5591–5606, 2016.

[9] D. Wu, D. I. Arkhipov, E. Asmare, Z. Qin, and J. A. McCann, "Ubiflow: Mobility management in urban-scale software defined iot," in *Computer Communications (INFOCOM), 2015 IEEE Conference on*. IEEE, 2015, pp. 208–216.

[10] J. Gubbi, R. Buyya, S. Marusic, and M. Palaniswami, "Internet of things (iot): A vision, architectural elements, and future directions," *Future generation computer systems*, vol. 29, no. 7, pp. 1645–1660, 2013.

[11] B. Bhushan and G. Sahoo, "Routing protocols in wireless sensor networks," in *Computational intelligence in sensor networks*. Springer, 2019, pp. 215–248.

[12] I. Snigdh and N. Gupta, "Quality of service metrics in wireless sensor networks: A survey," *Journal of The Institution of Engineers (India): Series B*, vol. 97, no. 1, pp. 91–96, 2016.

[13] Z. Ming and M. Yan, "A modeling and computational method for qos in iot," in *2012 IEEE International Conference on Computer Science and Automation Engineering*. IEEE, 2012, pp. 275–279.

[14] H. Mostafaei, "Energy-efficient algorithm for reliable routing of wireless sensor networks," *IEEE Transactions on Industrial Electronics*, vol. 66, no. 7, pp. 5567–5575, 2018.

[15] M. A. Razzaque, M. Milojevic-Jevric, A. Palade, and S. Clarke, "Middleware for internet of things: a survey," *IEEE Internet of things journal*, vol. 3, no. 1, pp. 70–95, 2015.

[16] S. Zafar, S. Jangsher, O. Bouachir, M. Aloqaily, and J. B. Othman, "Qos enhancement with deep learning-based interference prediction in mobile iot," *Computer Communications*, vol. 148, pp. 86–97, 2019.

[17] J. Ordonez-Lucena *et al.*, "Network slicing for 5g with sdn/nfv: Concepts, architectures, and challenges," *IEEE Communications Magazine*, vol. 55, no. 5, pp. 80–87, 2017.

[18] E. Coronado, S. N. Khan, and R. Riggio, "5g-empower: A software-defined networking platform for 5g radio access networks," *IEEE Transactions on Network and Service Management*, vol. 16, no. 2, pp. 715–728, 2019.

[19] H. Mostafaei and M. Menth, "Software-defined wireless sensor networks: A survey," *Journal of Network and Computer Applications*, vol. 119, pp. 42–56, 2018.

[20] N. Saha, S. Bera, and S. Misra, "Sway: Traffic-aware qos routing in software-defined iot," *IEEE Transactions on Emerging Topics in Computing*, p. 1, 2018.

[21] G.-C. Deng and K. Wang, "An application-aware qos routing algorithm for sdn-based iot networking," in *2018 IEEE Symposium on Computers and Communications (ISCC)*. IEEE, 2018, pp. 00 186–00 191.

[22] S. K. Tayyaba, M. A. Shah, O. A. Khan, and A. W. Ahmed, "Software defined network (sdn) based internet of things (iot): A road ahead," in *Proceedings of the International Conference on Future Networks and Distributed Systems*. ACM, 2017, p. 15.

[23] ONF, "Software-defined networking: The new norm for networks," Open Networking Foundation, Tech. Rep., April 2012. [Online]. Available: https://www.opennetworking.org/images/stories/downloads/sdn-resources/white-papers/wp-sdn-newnorm.pdf

[24] N. McKeown *et al.*, "Openflow: enabling innovation in campus networks," *ACM SIGCOMM Computer Communication Review*, vol. 38, no. 2, pp. 69–74, 2008.

[25] A. Shalimov *et al.*, "Advanced study of sdn/openflow controllers," in *Proceedings of the 9th central & eastern european software engineering conference in russia*. ACM, 2013, p. 1.

[26] G. Joel, "Data science from scratch," 2015.

[27] S. Song, J. Lee, K. Son, H. Jung, and J. Lee, "A congestion avoidance algorithm in sdn environment," in *2016 International Conference on Information Networking (ICOIN)*. IEEE, 2016, pp. 420–423.

[28] R. M. Karp, "Reducibility among combinatorial problems," in *Complexity of computer computations*. Springer, 1972, pp. 85–103.

QoS-Aware Adaptive Resource Allocation Framework in the Integrated SDN Transport and IoT

Atefeh Meshinchi
Polytechnique Montréal
Montreal, Canada
email: atefeh.meshinchi@polymtl.ca

Ranwa Al Mallah
Ryerson University
Toronto, Canada
email: ranwa.almallah@ryerson.ca

Alejandro Quintero
Polytechnique Montréal
Montreal, Canada
email: alejandro.quintero@polymtl.ca

***Abstract*—Internet of Things (IoT) is a key technological enabler to create smart environments and provide various benefits such as productivity improvement and business process cost minimization. For its successful deployment, various innovative applications are being developed in different IoT fields, each demanding various Quality of Service (QoS) requirements to achieve their desired objectives. In the context of a smart city, a huge number of IoT applications are being developed for emergency management operation (fire, flood, and earthquake) and city traffic congestion management. These applications require fast system reaction to get the valuable data and make appropriate decisions. Therefore, it is essential to design and develop a service model that ensures an appropriate level of QoS for such application. We propose a framework for QoS support in the IoT system considering the application specific QoS needs from the IoT networking subsystems such as the sensing and core transport networks. To achieve this, we take advantage of the Software-Defined Networking (SDN) technology integrated into the IoT system to provide a flexible and adaptive QoS-aware resource allocation scheme for IoT services. We put forward a programmable control layer to provide customized and generic support services for IoT applications.**

Keywords–Internet of Things; quality of service; software-defined Network; resource allocation.

I. INTRODUCTION

The Internet of Things (IoT) is the radical evolution of the current Internet into a network of interconnected objects. The IoT system is comprised of a large number of heterogeneous devices, and consequently diverse services and a multitude of applications. Each application requires a specific level of IoT system performance to operate appropriately and effectively. As a standard IoT architecture, multiple systems, such as devices, data, network and communication are involved in the fulfillment of the service [1].

Wireless Sensor Networks (WSNs), widely used in the IoT infrastructure, are comprised of hundreds of sensor nodes that provide the data for applications to be proceeded and transformed into useful outputs. Thus, the performance level of the services not only depends on the communication network (e.g., Internet), it also depends on the performance of the sensing network [2]. In comparison to Internet applications, which care about the performance of the data transmission services in terms of delay, loss rate, and bandwidth, Quality of Service (QoS) attributes, such as data accuracy and sampling rate are more valuable for IoT applications for service delivery [3].

Sensing nodes are generally low-end devices with strong constraints in energy, processing, storage, and transmission capabilities. Some sensors do not support the IP addressing scheme since implementation of the IP stack is resource-intensive and is too challenging in low-end devices. Therefore, the direct connection between applications and sensors cannot be established. An IoT gateway can act as a bridge between IP-based systems and non-IP sensors to facilitate data formatting and transmission. For cost efficiency, WSNs are generally designed as multi-service systems to be shared among multiple applications [4].

World-wide availability makes the Internet the best available option for inter-connectivity of IoT. However, the Internet enforces some challenges. In the legacy network, the control intelligence, which is implemented by various routing and management protocols, is embedded in every network element. Thus, vendor-dependent platforms and interfaces make the Internet evolution complex and slow. Also, the Internet provides best-effort services and is not capable to meet more specific requirements of applications in terms of service quality. In IoT, heterogeneous networks and devices create opportunities for a wide range of applications with very diverse QoS requirements, which may not be guaranteed by the best-effort Internet mechanisms [5]. On the other hand, Software Defined Networking (SDN) is a new paradigm for computer networking that appeared recently to break down the closeness of network systems in both control and data functions. SDN allows the network owners and administrators to programmatically initialize, control, and manage network behavior by decoupling the control plane from the data plane.

The Internet of Things is not a single technology like the Internet and it is compounded with many functions including sensing, processing, transmission, analysis, and deciding. So, many different technologies in terms of hardware, software, data, and communication are involved in the different layers of IoT architecture to implement the smart environments. Therefore, Quality of Service not only must be embedded in the production and design of all hardware and software components in IoT infrastructure, their integrations in the IoT system might raise needs for adaption and adjustment with the dynamic nature of IoT and application requirements. In other words, the overall IoT service quality and end-user satisfaction depend on various service providers like sensing service, network service, and cloud and it is carried out by all involved technologies and components of the IoT service.

Thus, the specific architecture would depend on the IoT application domains and the enabling technologies used in specific implementations.

Applications are fundamental to the IoT. They provide the presentation layer for the data captured from the billions of devices around the world. Unlike IT applications, IoT applications could be classified from different perspectives such as the type of information they manage, the type of recipient (person or system oriented), and their criticality. The IoT solution owner may define how the particular application must be treated from the QoS point of view depending on the business need. Besides, the growth of the innovative applications and their spontaneous deployment in the IoT system make the IoT Service Level Agreement (SLA) more dynamic and diverse. So, the application mission may vary over time regardless of the type of the traffic like data or voice which is the input for QoS classifiction in tradational IT environement. Apart from the flexibility and scalability of the IoT solutions, the simplicity of system control and management must be considered in the design of the solution so that IoT applications could be deployed easily and creatively.

The performance of an IoT application is impacted by the performance of the communication network and sensing data. Organizations need to design a flexible and scalable QoS framework to keep up with system growth, diverse application types and complexity of the system. To ensure that the system can provide the guaranteed service delivery, the QoS requirements of the application must be addressed at all involved subsystems and layers of the IoT architecture. In this paper, we aim to manage the IoT infrastructure resources to provide QoS support. To accomplish this goal, we integrate the SDN technology into IoT architecture to leverage SDN characteristics and features to design a QoS management framework, which could keep pace with innovative requirements of IoT application and support resource-dynamic environment. We propose a flexible and programmable control layer to provide customized and generic support services for the IoT applications.

The rest of the paper is organized as follows. In Section II, we provide a review of related studies that investigate different aspects of QoS in the IoT system. In Section III, we describe the proposed QoS support framework. Section IV details the framework workflow. Finally, in Section V, the primary conclusions and future work are outlined.

II. LITERATURE REVIEW

Various QoS factors need to be taken into account when designing IoT services. This is due to the IoT architecture that depends on multiple subsystems. Approaches must consider QoS needs across the multiple subsystems, the diversity of the application domains, the volume and variety of the devices. Some research focus on enhancing the QoS control and management within IoT subsystems. For WSNs, a main component of the IoT infrastructure, studies investigate into the QoS-based design in the aspects of the routing protocols, clustering, and topology update. Solutions differ on the design methodology and details of the quality factors. Energy, bandwidth efficiency, storage, coverage optimization, and data accuracy enhancement are mostly targeted in the research.

On the other hand, some studies focus on QoS support schemes and architecture and aim at measuring the QoS attributes necessary for QoS-aware service delivery. In [6], the authors model a sensor's quality of information including principles and policies to exchanging the quality-related metadata about the collected data. In [7], the authors consider data accuracy and latency to estimate the Quality of Information (QoI) from the end-user perspective. In [8], Irfan et al. perform an analytical model for application prioritization and scheduling in a finite-capacity queuing system considering application performance requirements. Authors in [9] introduce a broker-based QoS management framework across IoT architectural layer. Most of the approaches and frameworks proposed concentrate on one or multiple QoS factors within a particular IoT subsystem. The works seek optimized hardware designs, protocols and decision-making algorithms to monitor, design or manage particular QoS parameters in WSNs. The platforms have very high level design and do not consider the end to end QoS management within a closed IoT system.

In recent years, software-defined systems and the idea of having a programmable network gained more interest in the industry and research institutions [10]. SDN architecture is made up of three logical layers: the data, control and application layers. The communication between the forwarding devices in the data layer and the centralized controller in the control layer is done through newly designed interfaces known as southbound interfaces. OpenFlow is the first standard southbound interface. The control layer communicates with application layer through a Northbound interface. Northbound interface enable flexibility in the programming of business-specific needs and has a centralized control over the network elements. From this perspective, studies in the literature propose generic traffic engineering techniques or innovative QoS management applications in terms of resource reservation, routing, queuing, and policy enforcement [11].

Some studies apply SDN technology to cellular and wireless networks. Software Defined Wireless Network (SDWN) apppeared as a way to provide a unified control plane to manage dynamic and heterogeneous wireless technologies, such as WiFi, WiMAX, 3G, LTE, and 5G [12]. In [13], they focus on mobility management, leveraging SDN architecture and its application within heterogeneous wireless environments in data flow context. On the other hand, Software-Defined WSNs (SDWSNs) seek to apply the separation of the control plane and data plane to the WSN architecture and provide re-configurable sensors. However, heterogeneity, data-centric nature of WSNs, and lack of TCP/IP stack support make softwarization more challenging in WSNs [14]. The SDIoT framework model proposed in [15] offers a centralized control system over security, storage and infrastructure resources. Most proposals are conceptual and analytical models which target architecture and framework and they are not established so far since the design of the controller and the management application would be a very complex task considering scale and diversity of IoT device and application [16]. Thus, the concept of SD-IoT is in its infancy and standardization efforts in terms of framework, protocol, software-defined application and assessment tools are still underway.

As a more granular research in this domain, the authors in [17] proposed an intrusion detection solution within the SDN-based cloud IoT environment. They leverage a machine learning technique to analyse network flow statistics to detect anomalous actions. There have been various studies on applying SDN to 5G systems. As another use case, in industrial IoT solutions, the authors in [18] focus on failure occurrences and recovery management in smart grid networks by leveraging SDN controller and with the aid of real-time monitoring mechanisms to improve the system resiliency. They propose an SDN-based programmable platform to manage policies through a centralized controller within 5G Radio access elements by abstracting the heterogeneities in that layer. Unlike our work, most proposals are conceptual and analytical models which target architecture and framework and they are not established so far since the design of the controller and the management application would be a very complex task considering scale and diversity of IoT device and application. Some of the IoT enabling technologies like the Internet and the cellular access networks (e.g. 3G, LTE) have the evolved QoS functions within their closed systems. However, their integrations into IoT bring issues and limitations. With the realization of the 5G technology, the barriers of the access networks are rectified, since 5G provides less-delay and high-bandwidth access network for the IoT system. The Internet imposes some limitations in terms of the supported QoS mechanisms. Compared to web applications, IoT applications are of dynamic and data-centric nature and they would have diverse QoS needs. Therefore, current QoS differentiation mechanism could not meet the diverse and progressive QoS needs of the IoT applications.

In all the studies, SDN technology is being integrated into the closed environments such as WSNs and 5G networks to manage the resources based on their specific characteristic, and particular point of view like security and performance. In contrast, in our proposed framework, we aim to provide centralized and programmable middleware to manage resources within multi-layer IoT system in an end to end fashion. The framework provides a way to better-fit resources from multiple networkers like 5G, 4G, Internet, or/and WSNs serving particular application data by enabling end to end visibility and improving the resource management. We realized a lack of study in the field of performance management in which heterogeneous devices, network resources, and application needs could be controlled and managed in an easy and flexible way. In the next section, we propose a middleware-based and SDN-oriented QoS support framework for IoT application. The SDN technology is leveraged in the networking layer to provide a flexible and adaptive control on network resource allocation based on the application QoS requirements.

III. QoS Support Framework for IoT

The proposed framework, illustrated in Figure 1, consists of several databases and functional elements deployed in the different layers of the IoT architecture. We categorize the building blocks of proposed framework in infrastructure, control and application layers.

A. Application Layer

In the application layer, the framework is composed of two databases, which could be implemented in the cloud environment for scalability and high availability.

- *Global wireless sensing network Database*: This database includes the profiles of IoT WSNs, such as supported services, bandwidth, coverage information (location), and IP addresses of the IoT gateways used for intercommunication between WSNs and external IP network. These general information could be provided by the Sensing Network Provider (SNP) in the network deployment phase. Also, this database keeps the overall status of WSNs in terms of the energy residue level, sensor availability status, the quality level of the collected data (QoI), and the service cost at any given time. Dynamic characteristics of WSNs could be estimated over the time by the IoT-gateways based on the implemented algorithms. Figure 2 demonstrates a logical format of the WSN profiles and supporting services.
- *SLA-based application QoS Database*: In general, the performance aspects of the service in terms of QoS attributes expected by a customer is covered in the SLA. In the IoT system, SLA includes application QoS requirements from the communication and sensing networks. Either application owner or service provider can provide the QoS-relevant information based on the agreed SLA. Figure 3 demonstrates the logical format for the database.

B. Infrastructure Layer

The infrastructure layer includes the WSNs, IoT gateways, and the forwarding network. Forwarding elements are controlled by the network controller located in control layer and WSNs are controlled by the IoT-gateways. In the proposed framework, IoT gateways provide QoS-aware resource allocation and task scheduling within the local WSNs, through implemented algorithms and functions illustrated in Figure 4. *Sensors Status Collector* collects the status of the sensors in terms of availability, energy residue, and the quality level of collected data and updates *Sensors Status Database*. *QoS-aware Sensing Resources Allocator* allocates sensors for any IoT application considering the QoS and energy status of sensors stored in *Sensors Status Database*. *Active Demand Database* keeps the currently active service demand and relevant configuration setup. When a new request is received, IoT-gateway verifies this database to verify whether this demand is replicated or any current active demand could satisfy this new request.

The overall network lifetime and the quality of information are calculated by *WSN Energy Residue Calculator* and *WSN Quality Level Calculator* respectively, and then *Global wireless sensing network Database* are updated to keep most up-to-date information regarding sensor status.

Pre-scheduled Data Collection Setup includes application subscription information, predefined task and data collection setup in terms of QoS requirement, and this function is used when continuous data collection is needed by applications, so task setup is pre-scheduled in the gateway for efficiency and resource optimization purpose. The collected data could be stored either in the local or in the global storage.

C. Control Layer

The control layer consists of several functions implemented on top of the controller in the SDN network to handle QoS support routing management within the transport network. The building blocks and between-blocks relationships are illustrated in Figure 5.

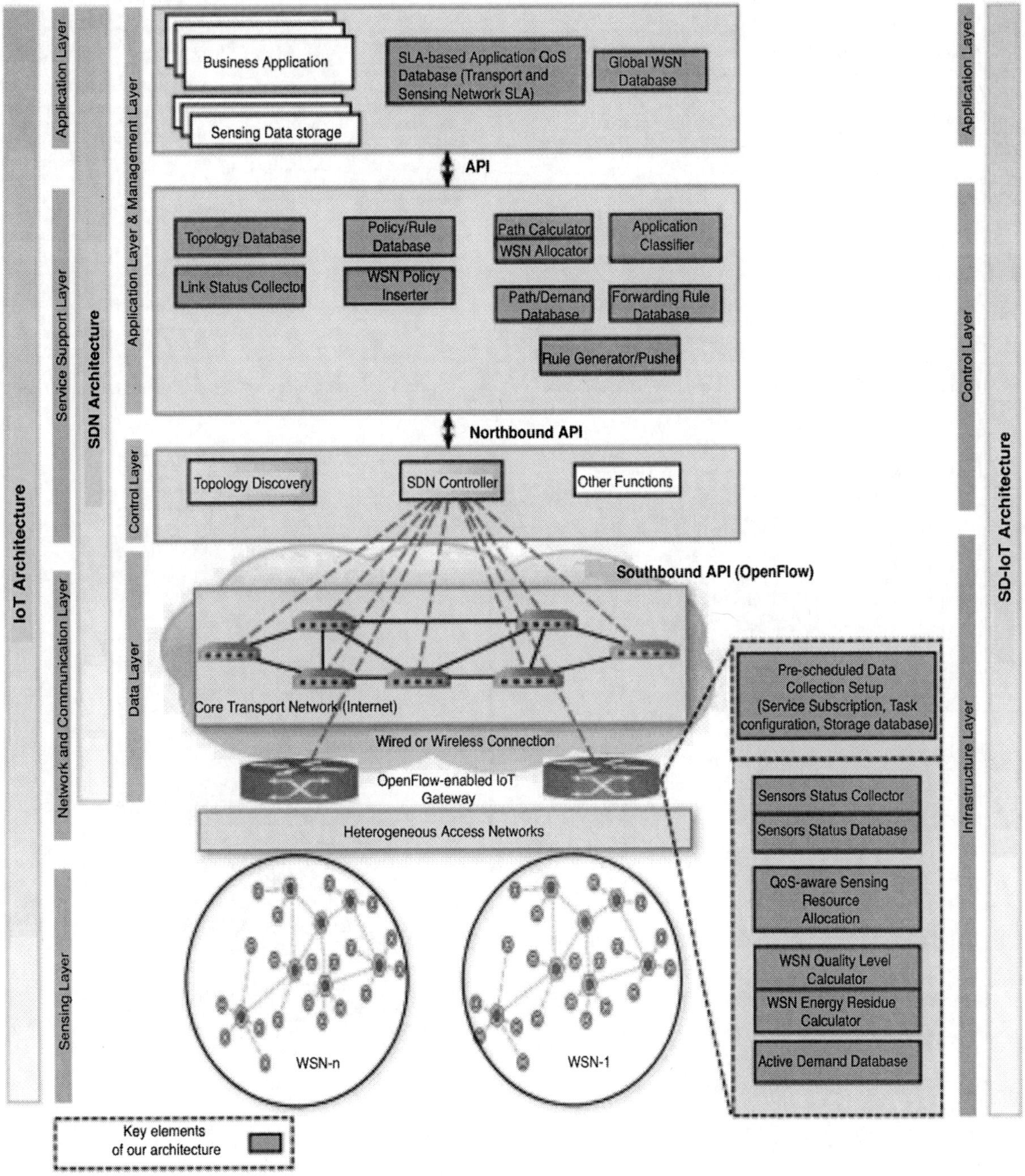

Figure 1. QoS framework for IoT through Transport SDN middleware.

According to the OpenFlow specification, the *Topology Discovery* function is implemented by default in the SDN-controller and enables the controller to discover the forwarding network topology. The controller discovers the network elements by exchanging HELLO messages and assessing their connection structures by the OpenFlow Discovery Protocol (OFDP) mechanism. The controller encapsulates an Link Layer Discovery Protocol (LLDP) packet as a packet-out message and sends it to the connected elements. The Network Element (NE) sends the received LLDP packet to all its neighbors which are connected directly to its active ports. A network element sends a received LLDP packet from another element to the controller as a Packet-in message since there is no matching entry in its Flow Table. The controller learns which network elements are connected directly to each other through received Packet-in messages and builds the global network physical

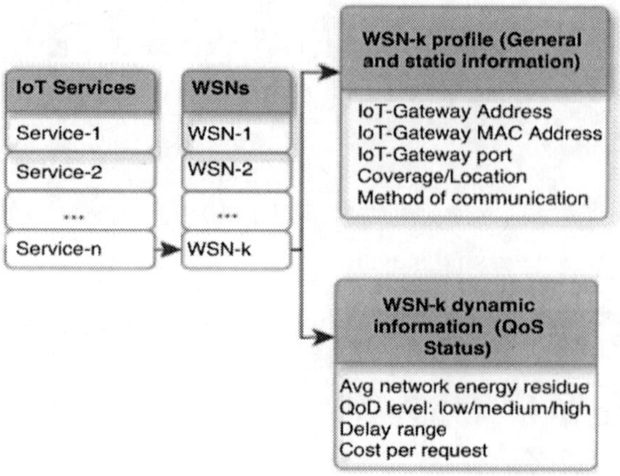

Figure 2. Logical format for Global sensing network Database.

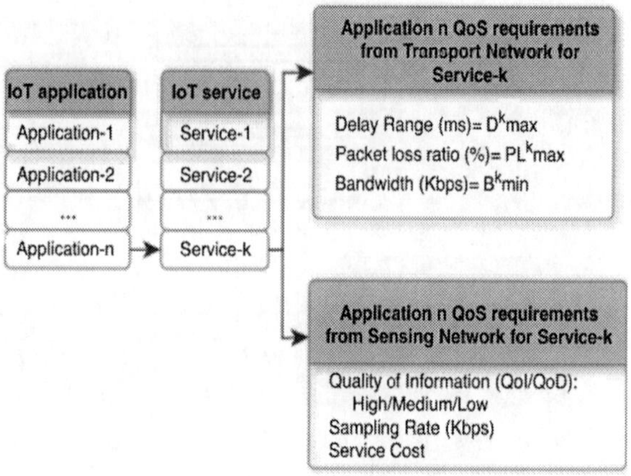

Figure 3. Logical format for IoT application SLA-based QoS Database.

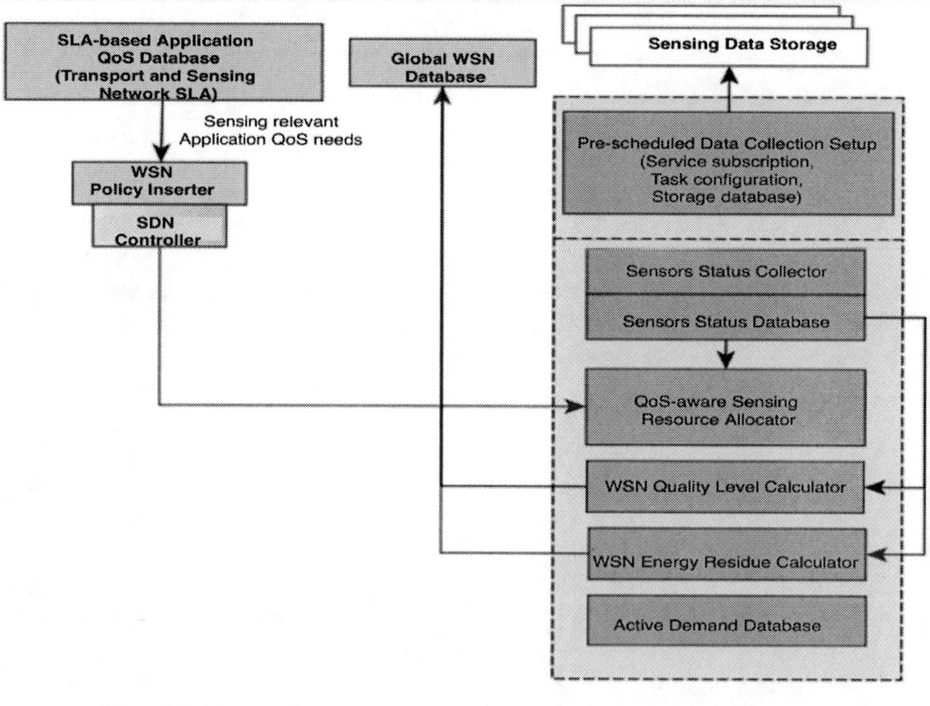

Figure 4. Infrastructure-layer components and their relationships within the framework.

topology [19].

Link Status Collector collects network performance parameters including the link packet loss ratio, bandwidth, and delay in real-time manner within the network topology discovered by *Topology Discovery* and stores the information in *Topology Database*.

As per the OpenFlow specification, several counters have been implemented in OpenFlow-enabled network elements to store packet processing records, such as flow, port, and queue [20]. They can be used to calculate the QoS parameters, such as link delay, link loss rate, and bandwidth. Flow-level counters provide information about a particular flow, e.g., a number of bytes forwarded, dropped, or erroneous and the duration of the flow to be delivered. Port-level counters provide more specific information about a particular port. Queue-level counters provide information about a particular queue attached to a particular output port.

In OpenFlow, for the traditional network, several tools have been developed to monitor and measure the network status, and they are classified in two big categories: passive or active monitoring [21]. The methods can be extended to the SDN and used in the implementation of the *Link Status Collector*. *Topology Database* is updated by both *Topology Discovery* and *Link Status Collector* periodically or in case of any changes in the network topology and link status, respectively.

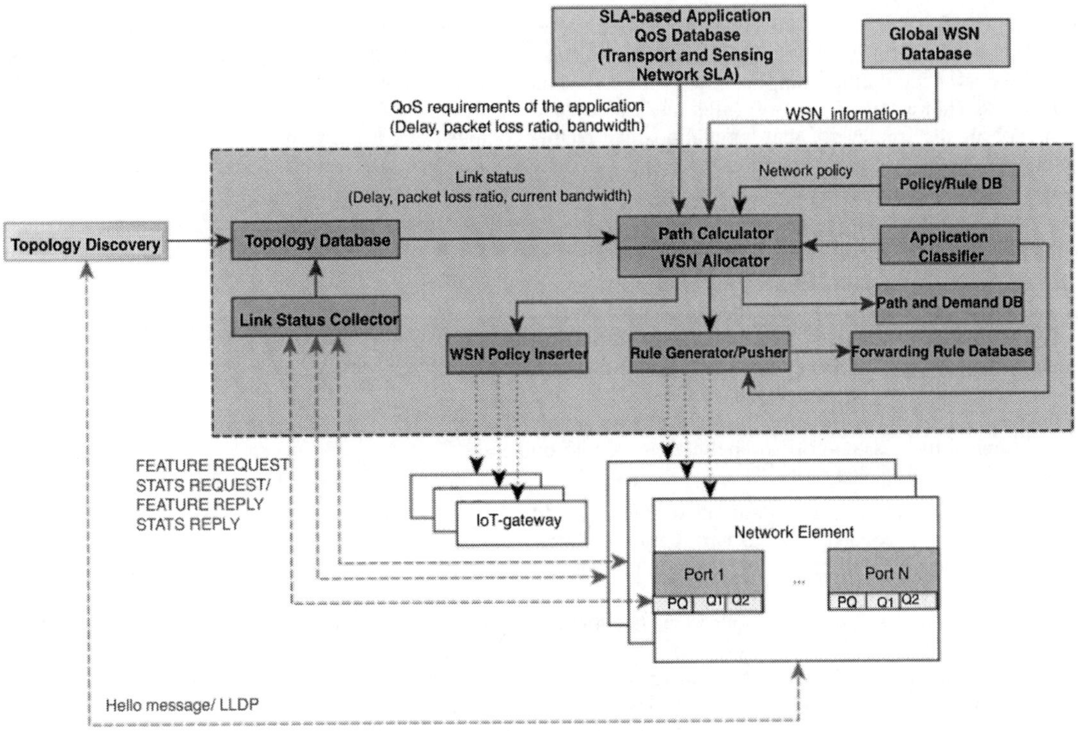

Figure 5. Control layer building blocks.

The messaging mechanisms in the OpenFlow protocol facilitates the communication between the *Link Status Collector* and the counters inside the network elements. FEATURE REQUEST/STATS REQUEST and FEATURE REPLY/STATS REPLY messages are used to request and return the value of counters respectively.

Policy/rule Database holds the network policy, such as bandwidth reservation, load balancing and admission control method to control the network resource allocation. The principles applied for network congestion or application preferences violation could also be kept in this database. The policy could be provided statically by network administrator or dynamically based on the network situations by the designed SDN application.

Application Classifier provides the application scheduling and prioritization within network elements. The default traffic scheduling algorithm implemented in the network elements is First-In First-Out where the traffic leaves the network element in the order in which they arrive. This method can not be suitable for an IoT environment since the scheduling algorithm does not take care of traffic QoS requirements and application class to prioritize them. Thus, mission-critical applications might experience non-acceptable delays or multimedia applications might not be served by proper capacity sharing. To provide a queuing mechanism as a fundamental scheduling technique in our framework, we classify IoT applications in three categories based on their sensitivity to delay and bandwidth: (1) control applications, also called mission-critical applications, such as city-traffic management and emergency management, which need very fast response with as less error as possible, (2) monitoring applications, such as intelligent security surveillance tasks, which are fed by cameras and need more throughput, and (3) analysis and inquiry applications, called general, such as the inquiry into the transported item state in the intelligent logistics, which are throughput and delay tolerant.

We propose three different queues in each port of the OpenFlow-enabled network elements: (1) Priority Queue (PQ) as the most prioritized queue includes mission-critical applications with intensive delay sensitivity. If the delay requirement of the application is less than a pre-defined threshold, it is marked as a high-prioritized demand and it is inserted in PQ of egress ports of network elements. (2) Q1 represents the data-centric application with bandwidth sensitivity, and less delay-sensitive compared to the pre-defined threshold. (3) Q2 contains applications with no strict QoS requirements, also called the best-effort application. Although queuing mechanisms guarantee the network bandwidth to the different applications, other techniques, such as *Complete Buffer Sharing* and *Preemptive Priority Scheduling* can also be implemented to minimize the network latency and increase efficiency of mission-critical applications.

Unlike IT applications which are categorized based on the type of traffic to which delay thresholds may be associated, IoT applications could be classified from different perspectives, such as the type of information they manage, the type of recipient (person or system oriented), and the criticality level of services they provide. Currently, IoT systems still suffer from the lack of standardized mechanisms to represent the diverse application requirements in order to be used as reference for our proposed model. Thus, such threshold do not exist. To setup the reasonable thresholds for QoS metrics, we plan to do experiments with multiple applications within an end to end deployed framework. It is only after an end to end implementation of the framework that simulations can enable us to gather data from production applications, and calculate the average value for the metric of delay threshold.

Moreover, in Complete Buffer Sharing scheme, the highest priority traffic push out the lower priority traffic. All packets in higher priority queue are served before a lower priority queue. In Preemptive Priority Scheduling, if a new process having a higher priority than the currently running process arrives, it gets selected immediately and the new process has not to wait until the currently running process finishes or yields. Having both mechanism in queue management would minimize the latency experienced by mission-critical applications served by the first queue in our proposed model.

A potential application of the three defined queues could be for instance in the context of a Smart City. A Smart City solution can leverage information and communication technologies to provide the critical infrastructure and services for city administration, transportation, education, health-care, public safety, and utilities. A City traffic and emergency management applications which need very fast response with as less error as possible, can be considered as delay-sensitive application served by PQ. Monitoring applications, such as intelligent security surveillance which are fed by cameras and need more throughput, can be classifed in Q1. Finally, analysis applications, such as the inquiry into the transported item state in the intelligent logistics, may be classifed as throughput and delay tolerant and may be pushed to Q2.

WSN Allocator determines the best-fit sensing network based on the current status of the WSNs (stored in *Global WSN Database* for the application request. *Path Calculator* queries the application QoS, policy and topology databases and calculate the SLA-respected routing path from the source of the demand to the IoT-gateway of the destination WSN for the application data-flow.

Rule Generator/Pusher translates the routing path made by *Path Calculator* into the actual configuration commands for each of the network elements. It generates the flow rules of the route information and configures the Flow Table of all elements along the paths. In OpenFlow channel, *FLOW MOD* message is used by the controller to add, delete, or modify the Flow Table entries in the network elements. *SET QUEUE/EN QUEUE* actions specify the particular queue in a particular port which the flow entry should be entered.

Path and Demand Database keeps the active application request and path associated to the request. When network topology or status is changed because of a fault or new design, *Path Calculator* verifies this database to determine whether any currently active path across the network is affected by this change. The new path is calculated for the impacted demands and re-installed in network elements. This database is updated based on the completion of the request and recalculation of the new path.

In OpenFlow, forwarding rules for all network-elements are kept in a data structure of the controller. In the proposed framework, *Forwarding Rule Database* keeps all active flow rules on the entire SDN network controlled by the controller. To have the optimized OpenFlow messaging, when *Rule Generator/Pusher* generates the rule based on the calculated path, it first verifies whether the associated flow rules exist in the Flow Table of the network element otherwise, the new flow entry is pushed in the network elements. To keep *Forwarding Rule Database* up-to-date, all the modification of the Flow Table entries must be reflected in this database. Therefore, the controller sends either an add or delete command, or receives the flow rule expiration notification from the network element, it modifies the database. To dynamically provide the sensing-related application QoS needs for the IoT-gateway, there could be two approaches. Whether IoT-gateway queries the SLA-based database to fetch the required information or *WSN policy pusher* enforce the required data in the OpenFlow-enabled IoT-gateway.

IV. Framework Workflow

We describe the workflow diagram within the proposed framework when an IoT service request is initiated by an application. There are three data delivery models in an IoT system: (1) Query-driven, where data is generated on demand, (2) Event-driven, where data is generated in response to an event, and (3) Continuous or time-based in which real-time data is generated continuously or periodically.

In query-driven model, pull approach is used for data collection so that all sensors are kept silent until a request arrives from the associated application. In our scheme, the service request is received by the QoS management module on top of the SDN controller. First, *Path Calculator/WSN Allocator* verifies the application subscription for the requested service through querying *SLA-based Application QoS Database*. If the application subscription is approved, energy-efficient WSN is nominated to serve the request based on the WSN status information in the *Global WSN Database*. Next step is the calculation of the optimized routing path across the core transport network between the application and IoT-gateway of the determined WSN. To calculate the path, the designed QoS support routing function takes into account the source and the destination of the data, the QoS requirements of the application, and performance status of network links.

Moreover, application QoS requirements from the WSN are deployed within the programmable IoT-gateway by the remote controller, so IoT-gateway could assign the sensor and schedule the task by applying the received QoS information in the resource allocation and routing algorithms. Figure 6 and Figure 7 summarize the flow of steps when the data collection request is initiated by a query-driven application in the proposed framework.

In the event-driven data model, the sensors are programmed to report the data only when an event of interest occurs. The data collection approach used for the event-driven application is called the push approach in which sensors pro-actively collect data, either data is stored in the pre-defined storage or data is sent to the application. Therefore, data flows from the sensing layer towards the application layer. When IoT-gateway receives the collected data, it sends the data transfer request to the controller. Again, the QoS management module on top of the controller verifies the requested QoS needs and calculates the routing path across the core transport network respecting its preferences and the network status.

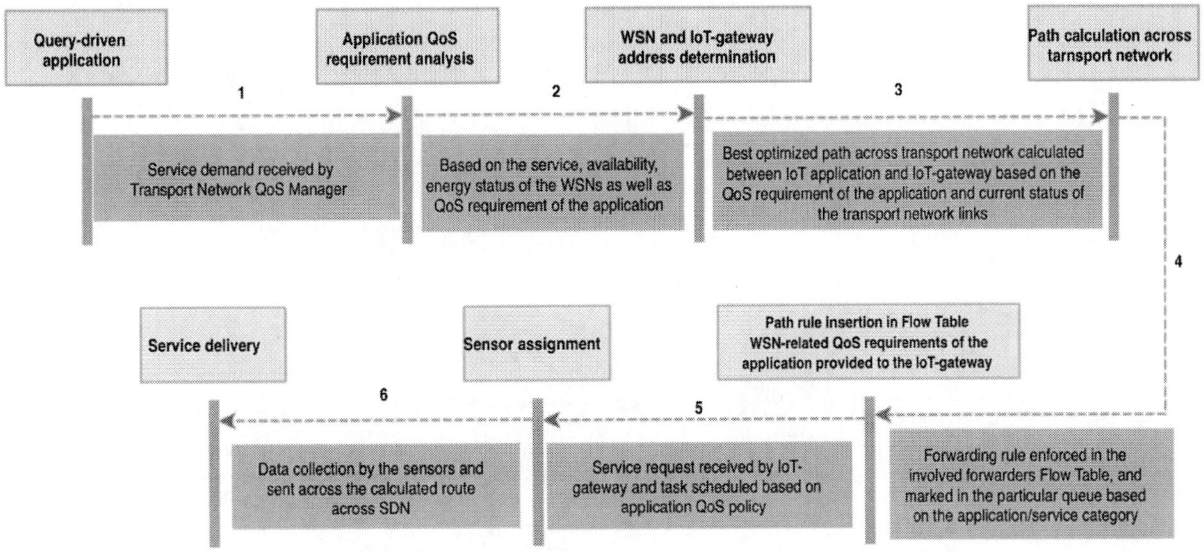

Figure 6. Sequence diagram when the proposed QoS support framework receives the service request from a query-driven IoT application.

Push approach could be more useful when multiple applications subscribe to the same data. To have a more efficient data collection process, *Prescheduled Data Collection Setup* provides the capability to publish data of subscribed applications so that applications could query the database and fetch the required data. In the continuous-based data model, same steps described for event-driven applications are followed to transfer the data from the IoT-gateway to the appropriate application server or database.

V. PERFORMANCE EVALUATION

We present the performance evaluation in terms of architectural, network and application perspective. We expand on the application of the proposed framework in the sections below by describing its characteristics and advantages from three perspectives.

A. Architectural perspective

The proposed framework has been mapped into both multilayer IoT architecture and SDN architecture. The SDN control layer/management layer provides a software layer between device and network infrastructures and applications. It works as the middleware and it enables the implementation of unified support services for the IoT system. In our design, the QoS module implemented over the controller provides the service support for QoS management in IoT framework: the end-to-end QoS routing across the SDN network, and QoS-aware sensing network allocation and sensor assignment. QoS needs of IoT application aims to be respected in each relevant layer, either core transport or sensing layer. Moreover, the resources and the routing path are allocated dynamically per-demand, depending on the specific service requirements and network resources status. Consequently, this design is adaptive to any changes in network and application QoS needs. The SDN northbound interfaces enable the enforcement of the quantified SLA-related QoS attributes directly in the resource allocation functions, which in the closed network is not possible due to the lack of such standard interfaces and programmable capabilities.

Since multiple programs could be implemented in the SDN controller, we are able to develop multiple algorithms and apply them in different conditions. We could use the best-effort routing path algorithm for the application class which has no strict QoS needs. For the QoS-based applications, a newly designed routing algorithm which considers the application constraint is applied. Since the framework uses the up-to-date information about the network status and application needs, it could provide the routing path dynamically over time.

Compared with the traditional QoS approaches such as IntServ and DiffServ, SDN-based core transport network resolves the limitation of the traffic differentiation and application classification according to their particular needs. As IoT system grows, it might bring the new class of applications with different QoS needs. Our architecture is flexible and fast-adapted based on the business needs. Applications can be classified to be treated differently regardless of the type of the traffic they process.

Based on the network resource status information and application request history captured by centralized SDN controller, it would be easier to learn the traffic pattern and predict the future traffic trend to extend the network based on business forecasts and avoid congestion. In fact, the authors in [22] proposed to leverage techniques based on artifical intelligence to resolve the resource management problem such as the traffic load prediction-based channel allocation problem to avoid traffic congestion. They propose a traffic load prediction-based adaptive channel assignment algorithm that aims to integrate SDN into IoT framework to improve the system control and management. The algorithm offers a centralized control system over security, storage and infrastructure resources. As a new algorithm, their work could be integrated into our proposed framework.

Implementing IoT data preprocessing and aggregation pro-

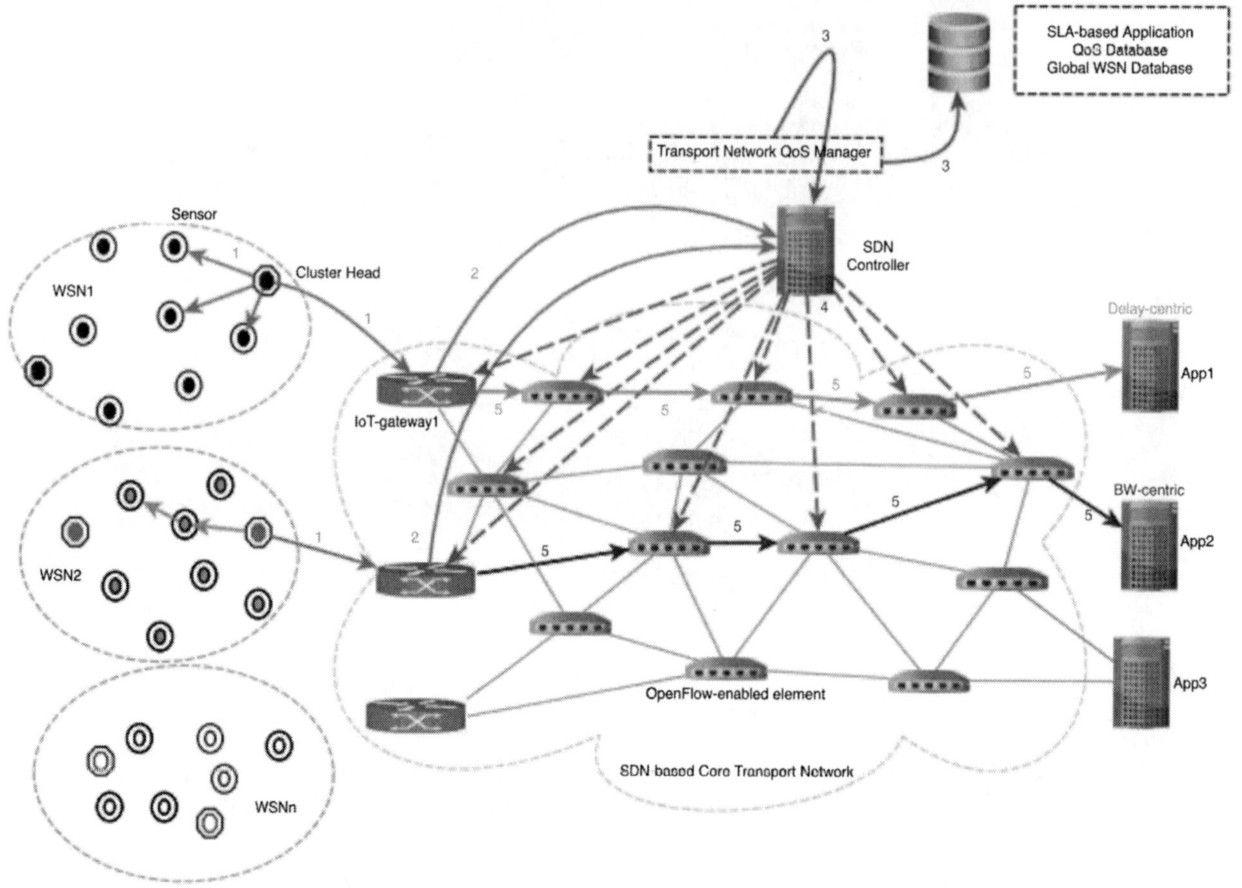

Figure 7. Mapping the steps into the framework components.

cess at the edge of the network within the local IoT-gateway not only enhances the transmission resource optimization and SDN network throughput, it speeds up the task scheduling and data acquisition for the user. The OpenFlow-enabled IoT-gateway also enables the sensing network programmability. The centralized algorithms and mechanisms in the IoT-gateway could be reprogrammed based on business and application needs, or when new optimized methods and solution are invented to manage the sensor resources in terms of clustering, routing, and task scheduling.

In [23], the authors proposed an SDN-capable IoT-GW that could facilitate the deployment of our proposed end to end QoS framework. We could leverage from the techniques of their study. With aid of specialized intelligent routing techniques developed in IoT gateways, wired and wireless devices could be managed in flexible and efficient way, although WSNs with low-end devices could be characterised and managed with a data-driven approach through centralized IoT-GW.

B. Network perspective

Network resource management in the globally distributed network such as transport network and the Internet is extremely complicated. One of the main benefits of the SDN-based core transport network is that it simplifies the network operation and management, compared with the traditional IP-based network which is defined in isolation and each vendor-dependent protocol only addresses a specific problem. We could leverage from SDN and its capabilities to develop customized network control and management services for core transport network. The controller as a centralized brain of SDN provides the single global map of the network and it abstracts the core transport network topology from the application layer. It enables the intelligent and agile decisions making regarding flow direction, control, and speedy network reconciliation when a link fails. The SDN controller can run multiple algorithms simultaneously in the field of network operation and maintenance. Therefore, network developer could deploy a wide range of the customized network application in terms of security, monitoring, performance management and fault-diagnosis. Also, scalability can be improved by centralizing the controller, where there is more global and less detailed view of the network elements.

Our framework dynamically collects the transport network topology and links status information. It increases the awareness of the network resource status at any given time. The design routing path excludes the higher utilized and congested links from the logical network topology when computing the route across SDN. It aims to make the link utilization balanced and it prevents the congestion probabilities in the transport network. It increases the transport network availability and accordingly, the IoT service availability. Suppose that the IoT sensing resources are available but the transport network is congested, it leads to failing the data transfer.

Furthermore, the centralized QoS management function does not deal with low-level configuration of data plane network elements. All the information such as SLA and network policy are specified in an abstracted level. Thus, reconfiguration of low-level settings in the network elements is not needed. All lead to saving a lot of resources, workforces and time.

C. Application perspective

IoT is placing new demands on network infrastructure due to the diverse application domain. With our proposed architecture, IoT applications can customize their own QoS requirements in terms of data acquisition and transmission. The designed path computation and QoS management functions compute a path with respect to the application QoS constraints which increases the user satisfaction, as well as, enabling of innovative application deployment.

Furthermore, using the queue policy to classify different applications based on their QoS needs and the operation criticality guarantees the quality of service for high priority demands when multiple demands fight for the available shared resources. Also, the collection of the current state of the network elements and being notified in case of changes or failure, these approaches help the SDN controller to be aware of the current network status and the occurred events such as link up/down or the node join/leave.

Network-state awareness and its involvement in the design of the routing computation algorithm decrease the possibility of link congestion and increase the network availability and throughput. Also, status-aware QoS-support resource allocation algorithm in sensing network fits the task and sensor data into application characteristic and needs. Additionally, the softwarization and centralization of the network services make the system to be in convergence with the changes. All of these approaches have an impact on the application satisfaction index (such as Quality of Experiences).

VI. Conclusion

The large number of IoT devices enable a wide variety of services in many different application domains, such as smart city, smart transport, smart home, and smart health. Each service and application depending on their goals and criticality may expect various QoS requirements from the IoT system in terms of data acquisition, transmission, and processing. There must be QoS approaches at every layer of the IoT architecture to ensure an acceptable level of performance especially for safety applications. We proposed a flexible and programmable control layer to provide customized and generic support services for the IoT applications. It is achieved by the integration of the core transport SDN into IoT architecture. We designed a status-aware and QoS-aware resource allocation framework across the IoT networking infrastructure. This framework has not been implemented in an end to end fashion due to the many underlying systems involved. Simulations must be planned in multiple phases. As a future work, we plan on simulating this framework in phases to account for the different technologies involved in the different layers of the IoT architecture. In our plan, the first step, QoS management in SDN-based network/Internet will be simulated considering the application QoS DBs as input. Afterwards, QoS management will be formularized for wireless network and broadband network (LTE). Finally, the end to end QoS calculation will be designed taking into account the underlying systems in the simulated environment. In another direction, we intend to model a status-aware and SLA-aware routing mechanism across the core transport software-defined network. Using different cost metrics for different application types, the model will find the less-delay and less-loss rate paths not only for delay-centric applications but also for bandwidth-centric applications.

References

[1] T. Kurakova, "Overview of the internet of things," Proceedings of the Internet of things and its enablers (INTHITEN), 2013, pp. 82–94.

[2] K. Mekki, E. Bajic, F. Chaxel, and F. Meyer, "A comparative study of lpwan technologies for large-scale iot deployment," ICT express, vol. 5, no. 1, 2019, pp. 1–7.

[3] D. Chen and P. K. Varshney, "Qos support in wireless sensor networks: A survey." in International conference on wireless networks, vol. 233, 2004, pp. 1–7.

[4] J. Gubbi, R. Buyya, S. Marusic, and M. Palaniswami, "Internet of things (iot): A vision, architectural elements, and future directions," Future generation computer systems, vol. 29, no. 7, 2013, pp. 1645–1660.

[5] A. Zanella, N. Bui, A. Castellani, L. Vangelista, and M. Zorzi, "Internet of things for smart cities," IEEE Internet of Things journal, vol. 1, no. 1, 2014, pp. 22–32.

[6] C. Bisdikian et al., "Building principles for a quality of information specification for sensor information," in 2009 12th International Conference on Information Fusion. IEEE, 2009, pp. 1370–1377.

[7] C. Bisdikian, L. M. Kaplan, and M. B. Srivastava, "On the quality and value of information in sensor networks," ACM Transactions on Sensor Networks (TOSN), vol. 9, no. 4, 2013, p. 48.

[8] I. Awan, M. Younas, and W. Naveed, "Modelling qos in iot applications," in 2014 17th International Conference on Network-Based Information Systems. IEEE, 2014, pp. 99–105.

[9] R. Duan, X. Chen, and T. Xing, "A qos architecture for iot," in 2011 International Conference on Internet of Things and 4th International Conference on Cyber, Physical and Social Computing. IEEE, 2011, pp. 717–720.

[10] K. M. Modieginyane, B. B. Letswamotse, R. Malekian, and A. M. Abu-Mahfouz, "Software defined wireless sensor networks application opportunities for efficient network management: A survey," Computers & Electrical Engineering, vol. 66, 2018, pp. 274–287.

[11] A. Mirchev, "Survey of concepts for qos improvements via sdn," Future Internet (FI) and Innovative Internet Technologies and Mobile Communications (IITM), vol. 33, no. 1, 2015, pp. 31–39.

[12] S. Costanzo, L. Galluccio, G. Morabito, and S. Palazzo, "Software defined wireless networks (sdwn): Unbridling sdns," in European workshop on software defined networking, 2012, pp. 1–6.

[13] H. Yang and Y. Kim, "Sdn-based distributed mobility management," in 2016 International Conference on Information Networking (ICOIN). IEEE, 2016, pp. 337–342.

[14] T. Miyazaki et al., "A software defined wireless sensor network," in 2014 International Conference on Computing, Networking and Communications (ICNC). IEEE, 2014, pp. 847–852.

[15] Y. Jararweh et al., "Sdiot: a software defined based internet of things framework," Journal of Ambient Intelligence and Humanized Computing, vol. 6, no. 4, 2015, pp. 453–461.

[16] S. K. Tayyaba, M. A. Shah, O. A. Khan, and A. W. Ahmed, "Software defined network (sdn) based internet of things (iot): A road ahead," in Proceedings of the International Conference on Future Networks and Distributed Systems. ACM, 2017, p. 15.

[17] T. G. Nguyen et al., "Search: A collaborative and intelligent nids architecture for sdn-based cloud iot networks," IEEE access, vol. 7, 2019, pp. 107 678–107 694.

[18] S. Al-Rubaye, E. Kadhum, Q. Ni, and A. Anpalagan, "Industrial internet of things driven by sdn platform for smart grid resiliency," IEEE Internet of Things Journal, vol. 6, no. 1, 2017, pp. 267–277.

[19] F. Pakzad, M. Portmann, W. L. Tan, and J. Indulska, "Efficient topology discovery in software defined networks," in 2014 8th International Conference on Signal Processing and Communication Systems (ICSPCS). IEEE, 2014, pp. 1–8.

[20] O. S. Specification, "Open networking foundation," Version ONF TS-015, vol. 1, no. 3, 2013, pp. 1–164.

[21] V. Mohan, Y. J. Reddy, and K. Kalpana, "Active and passive network measurements: a survey," International Journal of Computer Science and Information Technologies, vol. 2, no. 4, 2011, pp. 1372–1385.

[22] F. Tang, Z. M. Fadlullah, B. Mao, and N. Kato, "An intelligent traffic load prediction-based adaptive channel assignment algorithm in sdn-iot: A deep learning approach," IEEE Internet of Things Journal, vol. 5, no. 6, 2018, pp. 5141–5154.

[23] M. Ojo, D. Adami, and S. Giordano, "A sdn-iot architecture with nfv implementation," in 2016 IEEE Globecom Workshops (GC Wkshps). IEEE, 2016, pp. 1–6.

Identifying Long-Term Risks of the Internet of Things

Erik Buchmann

Hochschule für Telekommunikation Leipzig,
Gustav-Freytag-Str. 43-45, 04277 Leipzig, Germany
Email: buchmann@hft-leipzig.de

Andreas Hartmann

Hochschule für Telekommunikation Leipzig,
Gustav-Freytag-Str. 43-45, 04277 Leipzig, Germany
Email: hartmann@hft-leipzig.de

***Abstract*—The Internet of Things is a result of decades of research in Ubiquitous Computing and Mobile Computing. It comes with many advantages for businesses, industry and consumers. Typical examples are a seamless integration of physical objects into digital workflows and improved modes of use for consumer products. However, if non-smart devices are replaced by smart ones, the integrated IT components might generate new risks that stem from different lifecycles of embedded software, libraries and protocols used, and the IT ecosystem needed. We strive for an exhaustive catalog of long-term risks for the operational life-span of smart devices. To this end, we describe an approach to identify risks which might materialize years after a smart device has been rolled out and purchased. Furthermore, we present the risks for a fragment of a smart device's ecosystem we have identified so far.**

***Index Terms*—Internet of Things; Security; Risk Management**

I. Introduction

In the last years, advances in hard- and software in the area of Ubiquitous Computing and Mobile Computing have led to numerous industrial components and consumer products that have been equipped with sensors, computational resources and communication interfaces, e.g., to cloud services. Together, such smart devices form the Internet of Things (IoT) [1]. In many cases, smart devices stem from non-smart predecessors. For example, a modern smart TV looks and feels mainly like a classical non-smart one with some extras.

Using smart devices comes with a plethora of benefits. From a business perspective, IoT technology promises to reduce process costs, increase process speeds, allow for in-depth process monitoring or new options to integrate logistics processes or manufacturing processes with business activities. For consumers, IoT allows to create smart homes with devices that can be controlled remotely via smartphone, adapt to the user's habits, and provide convenient services locally or over the Internet. However, public and specialized media provides anecdotal evidence that smart devices might come with operational risks that appear after roll-out. With a familiar non-smart device in mind, the customers might not expect such risks when deciding for a smart device.

Example 1: Software and hardware lifecycles are different. *The device's software lifecycle might be much shorter than the hardware's operational capability. Consider a smart TV based on the Android TV operating system. Its software receives security updates for about three years. Thus, after three years the smart TV becomes a security issue [2], even if the hardware is still in good condition and fully operational.*

Example 2: Loss of control. *Smart devices may depend on a cloud service. For example, after a third-party service provider stopped its business, tens of thousands smart Internet radios became non-functional [3] without warning in advance.*

Example 3: Changing compliance or legislation. *Changes in the legislation may restrict the use of smart devices after years of operation. Consider a smart security camera generates burglar alerts via cloud service in the UK. Under the ongoing discussion of the Brexit [4] and the EU General Data Protection Regulation [5] (GDPR), it remains unclear under which conditions person-related videos can be sent to a cloud in the UK.*

In order to make smart devices accessible for risk management approaches, a comprehensive catalog of potential risks is required. However, to the best of our knowledge, existing approaches don't focus on long-term operations and have a narrow topic, e.g., IT security. We are interested in risks that materialize years after a smart device has been purchased. Thus, we define our problem statement as follows:

Which specific risks for the continued long-term use of smart devices may materialize after purchase, but cannot be expected from a smart device's non-smart predecessor?

We call an appliance a "smart device", if it contains computational capabilities and data links, which were not needed for the primary function of its non-smart predecessor. For example, a classical TV did not need Internet access to display live TV programmes. With "long-term" we refer to the operational time that can be expected from the device's hardware. Intuitively, this is the expectation of a naive customer who replaces a broken non-smart device with a new smart one.

In this paper, (1) we propose a research approach to systematically derive such risks, and (2) we exemplary outline the risks we have identified for one fragment of a smart device's infrastructure.

Paper outline: In Section II, we briefly discuss related work. In Section III, we sketch our approach to identify long-term IoT risks. In Section IV, we describe risks we have identified. Section V concludes.

II. Related Work

a) Risk Analyses for IoT: Advances in technology call for risk analysis before adoption. However, all risk analysis approaches we are aware of focus on the current situation and have a narrow perspective, e.g., on current IT security or return of investment. For example, [6] provides an exhaustive view on the vulnerabilities of smart devices in the consumer market. The risk assessment approach described in [7] considers the management of risk in the past two years, but does not feature a projection in the future, e.g., when security breaches for a discontinued product remain untreated. In consequence, existing approaches that deal with IoT risks over the product lifetime [8], [9] don't consider that vendors may loose interest in supporting discontinued products, or that it will be hard to find experts to maintain outdated technology.

b) Design Science Research: Design science research [10] is a method where an artefact is constructed from a knowledge base, evaluated and improved in multiple rounds. Those rounds can be structured in three cycles of activities. The *relevance cycle* specifies and refines the use cases needed to construct the artefact and to evaluate its applicability. The *rigor cycle* builds a knowledge base from literature and experience that is needed to evaluate the novelty and research contribution of the artefact. The central *design cycle* iterates between building and evaluating the artefact, based on information from the other cycles.

c) BSI-Standard 200-3: The BSI-Standard 200-3 [11] for risk analysis based on IT-Grundschutz defines a process that allows organizations to assess their information security risks. For this purpose, the standard defines the steps necessary for risk identification, risk assessment and risk treatment. In this paper we focus on risk identification. The standard separates (a) non-specific, elementary threats, as fire, theft, misconfiguration or manipulation, and (b) specific threats arising from specific scenarios. Furthermore, the standard provides the means for risk classification and consolidation.

d) Long-Term Digital Preservation: A problem that has been extensively discussed in the past years is the preservation of digital contents over time [12]. The risks for digital content [13] overlap with the risks of using an out-of-date smart device in a modern environment. Examples are media obsolescence and format obsolescence [13], i.e., the digital object cannot be read with current devices due new media or new formats. Security properties have been established with protocols that are insecure now [14]. Digital objects such as dynamic web pages [15] or computer games [16] require a complex execution environment.

III. How to identify Long-Term IoT risks

In this section, we describe our research method. To systematically identify long-term risks for the use of smart devices, we have adapted BSI-Standard 200-3 [11] so that it creates the knowledge base and designs a risk catalog that fits into relevance and design cycle of Design Science Research [10]. We use research literature to foster the rigor cycle. In particular, we define the following steps:

1) Determine a number of relevant use cases. On this basis, model a generic IT infrastructure that fulfils the requirements for a smart device and its non-smart counterpart to operate as intended.
2) Analyse each artefact in the infrastructure for the smart device in isolation. Determine under which conditions this artefact operates as intended at time of purchase.
3) Consider this condition a potential risk, if the condition doesn't exist at time of purchase and doesn't materialize in the non-smart device's infrastructure.
4) Consolidate risks that are identical for multiple artefacts. Categorize similar risks and remove elementary ones.
5) Back up each individual risk by literature in order to evaluate the plausibility of the risks identified.
6) Repeat these steps with different use cases until no further risks are identified.

For illustration, we apply this approach to Example 3 from the introduction. *Step 1:* The generic IT infrastructure for the smart security camera contains, among other things, a data connection between the smart device and a cloud service provider in the UK. This is because the security camera vendor has outsourced the burglar alert into the cloud. The connection transports personal data, e.g., videos of humans. *Step 2:* One required condition is that the data transfer is legal - depending on the legislation. *Step 3:* A common non-smart security camera uses a local storage system, not needing a legal authorisation for cross-border data transfers. *Step 4:* "Changing privacy legislation for data transfers into other countries" is not an elementary risk. *Step 5:* A body of literature can be identified, discussing the risks of changes in the privacy regulations for transferring data to a UK cloud, e.g., [4]. Thus, we have identified "changing privacy legislation" as a plausible risk for *any* smart device that uses such an IT infrastructure to transfer personal data.

IV. Categories of long-term risks

In this section, we describe the outcomes of our ongoing research according to the six steps defined in Section III.

a) Use Cases and IT Infrastructure Model: According to Step 1 of our research method, we started our analysis by determining a set of relevant use cases. To this end, we have selected three smart devices that have different purposes:

- A **smart TV** (Philips Ambilight 32PFS6402),
- a **smart security camera** (Reolink RLC-410) and
- a **smart speaker** (Amazon Echo) with voice assistant.

Following our method, we created a generic IT infrastructure model from those use cases. Our model considers data, organizations, processes, devices and connections.

TABLE I. Categories of data.

Id	*Name*	*Description*
D1	Sensor Data	Raw sensor information, such as unprocessed video and audio feeds, GPS and WLAN localization data or keystrokes from a remote control.
D2	Operational Data	Data needed to execute the device's function, e.g., commands to activate the smart speaker or a live video stream from the camera.
D3	Meta-Data	Time stamps, transmission information, character encoding, session keys etc. from the algorithms and protocols used.
D4	Configuration	Data that defines the behavior of the device, including updates, private keys and certificates.
D5	Telemetry	Data used to supervise the behavior and use of the device.

Table I contains the categories of data of our infrastructure model. We consider D1 - D5 as personal data according Art. 4 No. 1 GDPR [5]. A time series of D1, D2, D3 or D5 allows to construct a fingerprint of the device and/or of the user's activities. D4 contains unique logins for cloud services and personal settings. Thus, a relation to a single person can be determined, even there are no personally identifiable information generated, such as user name or image.

TABLE II. Categories of organizations.

Id	*Name*	*Description*
O1	User	The user of the smart device.
O2	Vendor	The vendor of the device.
O3	Cloud	The provider and operator of the cloud service.
O4	External	Any third party.

Table II describes the categories of organizations our model considers. Service operation may vary between O2 (Infrastructure as a Service) or O3 (Software as a Service). With O4 we refer to any external party that is invoked from the smart device. For example, Amazon's smart speaker can access the Google calendar or a Philips smart light bulb.

TABLE III. Categories of processes, assigned with data.

Id	*Name*	*Data*	*Description*
P1	Updates	D2, D3, D4, D5	All functional updates and security updates.
P2	Local Ops	D1, D2, D3, D4	Any operation that is processed locally on the device.
P3	Cloud Ops	D1, D2, D3, D4, D5	Any operation that is processed remotely in the cloud.
P4	External Ops	D1, D2, D3	Any operation that is processed by a third party.
P5	Telemetry	D3, D4, D5	The vendor supervising the behavior of the smart device.

The categories of processes are listed in Table III, together with the categories of data used. A process activity can be initiated by a local operation (P2), handed over for analysis to the cloud service (P3) and is executed as an external operation (P4). For example, an Amazon Echo recognizes the activation code "Hi Alexa" locally and sends an audio feed containing the sentence "Turn on all lights." to the Amazon cloud. The Amazon cloud service performs natural language processing, recognizes the commands and sends them to a Philips cloud service. Then, the Philips service activates the local light bulbs.

TABLE IV. Categories of devices, assigned with organizations.

Id	*Name*	*Organization*	*Description*
G1	Device	O1	The smart device itself.
G2	Cloud	O2, O3	The cloud service.
G3	ext. Device	O1, O3, O4	Any external device.

Table IV contains the categories devices and the organizations operating them. We have left aside the router needed to connect the smart device to the Internet. Our risk identification process has shown that any risk involving the router is an unspecific elementary risk. With "external Device" we refer to any situation where a third device is involved. This might be the user's smartphone, a virtual gadget in the cloud that is operated by a third party, or a smart home installation that is under control of the smart device.

TABLE V. Categories of connections, assigned with data.

Id	*Devices*	*Data*	*Description*
C1	G1 – G2	D1, D2, D3, D4, D5	Bidirectional connection: smart device– cloud.
C2	G2 – G3	D1, D2, D3	Bidirectional connection: cloud – external device.

Finally, Table V enumerates the categories of connections between the devices and the data transferred with each connection. If earphones, external storage, etc. is connected to the smart device, the associated risks are identical for smart and non-smart devices. Our use cases don't allow a direct connection between the smart device and an external device beyond that. For the time being, we assume any data transfer to an external recipient is managed by a cloud service.

b) Long-term risks for C2: Steps 2 to 5 of our research method let us identify and consolidate the long-term risks for each component of our infrastructure model. Furthermore, we have to filter risks that are specific for smart devices, and we need to substantiate them with literature. For the sake of brevity, we exemplary describe only the risks we have identified for the connection between the cloud service and an external device (Artefact C2). For each risk, we present only one example from literature to confirm it's existence.

After having consolidated the risks according to Step 4, we have learned that C2 has risks in three different areas. Table VI shows the compliance risks we have identified, Table VII contains the economic risks, and Table VIII lists the operational risks.

TABLE VI. Long-term compliance risks associated with C2.

Risk	*Description*
Legislation	Changing legislation, new codes of conduct, new trade restrictions etc. impose limitations on the exchange of personal data with certain countries or parties [4].
Expiration	Disagreements to common compliance standards, expired certifications or approvals, non-renewed audits, etc., render the connection untrusted [17].
Concealment	Characteristics that were hidden at roll-out ban the connection by law, e.g., if it becomes known that personal information is sent to external parties without the customers consent [18].

TABLE VII. Long-term economic risks associated with C2.

Risk	*Description*
Degradation	For economic reasons the service quality of the connection will be reduced, e.g., by applying bandwidth throttling in favor of other services [19].
Licensing	The revenue model might change. For example, the external party might switch to a pay-per-use model which makes external connections expensive [20].
Discontinuation	One of the parties involved discontinues its service or makes it uneconomic. Patents, licenses etc. disallow to continue the service with other parties [21].
Liabilities	One of the parties involved discontinues its business, and its contractual liabilities become void [22].

TABLE VIII. Long-term operational risks associated with C2.

Risk	*Description*
Inflexibility	Without updates for new formats, protocols or interfaces, it becomes challenging to connect to more recent services or devices, or to adapt to new modes of service [23].
Unreliability	The service level in terms of reliability, throughput, etc. of the connection degrades, e.g., due to reduced support for end-of-lifetime products [24].
Unmaintainability	Due to the use of outdated formats, protocols or interfaces and closed-source components it becomes difficult to find experts or spare parts needed to that maintain the connection [25].
Insecurity	Without security updates and by using out-of-date security protocols, the connection does not meet the required level of security any more [24].
Defectiveness	Modernizations in the IT ecosystem make technical debts visible, e.g., if header fields reserved for future use in transmission protocols were not handled according to the standard [26].

Recall that the tables contain the long-term risks for C2. An example for a risk for other fragments (G1–G3) is the absence of experts for today's high-tech components, that are outdated in the future. Every year, employees with expert knowledge retire, but new starters do not learn to use out-of-date technology. Considering the innovation cycles, this will become an issue when operating smart devices in the future.

As part of our ongoing research, we will follow the steps listed in Section III. We strive to identify a comprehensive set of long-term risks for all infrastructure artefacts from all categories. For this purpose, we will identify and consolidate such risks for all artefacts of our infrastructure model, and we will extend the model by further smart devices.

V. Conclusion

The Internet of Things is a promising approach from the area of Ubiquitous Computing and Mobile Computing to integrate physical objects into computing environments. However, if non-smart devices are replaced by smart IoT devices, the integrated IT components might generate new risks that stem from different lifecycles of digital and physical objects, and the IT ecosystem needed.

In this paper, we have developed an approach to identify risks which might materialize years after the purchase of a smart device. Furthermore, we described the risks we have identified for a fragment of a smart device's ecosystem. It is part of our future work to compile an exhaustive catalog of long-term risks for the operational life-span of smart devices.

References

[1] L. Atzori, A. Iera, and G. Morabito, "The internet of things: A survey," *Computer networks*, vol. 54, no. 15, pp. 2787–2805, 2010.

[2] B. Schoon, "Android tv needs better standards for long-term updates and support," https://9to5google.com/2019/08/29/android-tv-long-term-updates-support/, 2019, retrieved: 2020-06-09.

[3] Frontier Nuvola Support, "Why did the service change on the 7th may 2019?" https://srsupport.frontier-nuvola.net/portal/kb/articles/service-change, 2019, retrieved: 2020-06-10.

[4] K. McCullagh, "Brexit: potential trade and data implications for digital and fintech industries," *International Data Privacy Law*, vol. 7, no. 1, p. 3, 2017.

[5] Council of the European Union, "Regulation (eu) 2016/679 on the protection of natural persons with regard to the processing of personal data and on the free movement of such data," OJ L 119, 4.5.2016, p. 1–88, 2016.

[6] T. Alladi, V. Chamola, B. Sikdar, and K.-K. R. Choo, "Consumer iot: Security vulnerability case studies and solutions," *IEEE Consumer Electronics Magazine*, vol. 9, no. 2, pp. 17–25, 2020.

[7] M. Aydos, Y. Vural, and A. Tekerek, "Assessing risks and threats with layered approach to internet of things security," *Measurement and Control*, vol. 52, no. 5-6, pp. 338–353, 2019.

[8] O. Garcia-Morchon *et al.*, "A comprehensive and lightweight security architecture to secure the iot throughout the lifecycle of a device based on himmo," in *Symposium on Algorithms and Experiments for Wireless Sensor Networks*, 2015.

[9] J. L. Hernández-Ramos, J. B. Bernabé, and A. Skarmeta, "Army: architecture for a secure and privacy-aware lifecycle of smart objects in the internet of my things," *IEEE Communications Magazine*, vol. 54, no. 9, pp. 28–35, 2016.

[10] A. Hevner and S. Chatterjee, "Design science research in information systems," in *Design research in information systems*. Springer, 2010, pp. 9–22.

[11] Bundesamt für Sicherheit in der Informationstechnik, "BSI Standard 200-3: Risk Analysis based on IT Grundschutz," *https://www.bsi.bund.de*, 2017, retrieved: 2020-08-08.

[12] Digital Preservation Coalition, "Digital preservation handbook," https://www.dpconline.org/handbook, 2015, retrieved: 2020-06-09.

[13] S. Vermaaten, B. Lavoie, and P. Caplan, "Identifying threats to successful digital preservation: the spot model for risk assessment," *D-lib Magazine*, vol. 18, no. 9/10, pp. 1–21, 2012.

[14] H. M. Gladney, "Trustworthy 100-year digital objects: Evidence after every witness is dead," *ACM Transactions on Information Systems (TOIS)*, vol. 22, no. 3, pp. 406–436, 2004.

[15] G. TRUMAN, "Web archiving environmental scan: Harvard library report," *Digital Access to Scholarship at Harvard*, 2016.

[16] J. Andersen, "Where games go to sleep: the game preservation crisis," https://www.gamasutra.com/view/feature/134653/where_games_go_to_sleep_the_game_.php, 2011, retrieved: 2020-06-09.

[17] Y. T. Mak, S. Carr, and J. Needham, "Differences in strategy, quality management practices and performance reporting systems between iso accredited and non-iso accredited companies," *Management Accounting Research*, vol. 8, no. 4, 1996.

[18] J. C. Roberts and W. Al-Hamdani, "Who can you trust in the cloud? a review of security issues within cloud computing," in *Information Security Curriculum Development Conference*, 2011, pp. 15–19.

[19] D. A. Lyons, "Net neutrality and nondiscrimination norms in telecommunications," *Arizona Law Review*, vol. 54, p. 1029, 2013.

[20] M. A. Cusumano, "The changing software business: Moving from products to services," *Computer*, vol. 41, no. 1, pp. 20–27, 2008.

[21] M. A. Lemley and T. Simcoe, "How essential are standard-essential patents," *Cornell Law Review*, vol. 104, p. 607, 2018.

[22] A. Schwartz, "Products liability, corporate structure, and bankruptcy: toxic substances and the remote risk relationship," *Journal of Legal Studies*, vol. 14, no. 3, pp. 689–736, 1985.

[23] P. Mutchler *et al.*, "Target fragmentation in android apps," in *IEEE Security and Privacy Workshops*. IEEE, 2016, pp. 204–213.

[24] B. Ford, "Icebergs in the clouds: the other risks of cloud computing," in *4th USENIX conference on Hot Topics in Cloud Computing*, 2012.

[25] L. M. D. Ferreira, A. Arantes, and C. Silva, "Discontinued products," in *Conference on Operations Research and Enterprise Systems*, 2017.

[26] P. Kruchten, R. L. Nord, and I. Ozkaya, "Technical debt: From metaphor to theory and practice," *IEEE Software*, vol. 29, no. 6, pp. 18–21, 2012.

The Need of Proper Programming Models for CPS

Martin Richter, Christine Jakobs, Matthias Werner
Operating Systems Group
Chemnitz University of Technology
09111 Chemnitz, Germany
email: {martin.richter, christine.jakobs, matthias.werner}@informatik.tu-chemnitz.de

***Abstract*—Mobile cyber-physical systems consist of possibly moving heterogeneous execution units, which interact with their environment through sensors and actuators. Programming such systems without taking motion into account has already proven to be error-prone and complex, as challenges like communication or programming multiple different devices have to be considered by the developer. Corresponding programming models abstract from these challenges through the provision of transparencies. This allows the programmer to focus on describing the behavior of the system instead of managing its infrastructure. When mobility is taken into account, the devices tasks may depend on their positions in space. Therefore, location and motion awareness have to be supplied. This impedes the provision of distribution transparency, as the programmer has to consider the movement and positioning of certain objects. In contrast to supporting awareness, providing motion and location transparency allows to maintain distribution transparency. In exchange, this limits the developers ability to consider the positioning and movement of the devices. Therefore, a programming model, which bridges the gap between maintaining transparencies and providing awareness is required to enable the developer to focus on describing the behavior of the possibly mobile system as a whole. This paper aims to show that there is a need for research on such models. To achieve this goal, a systematic literature review is performed. Its main target is the assessment of existing programming models, regarding their provided types of awareness and transparency. To classify on which aspects of the system the considered programming models focus, an architectural model for mobile cyber-physical systems is introduced. Additionally, desired programming model properties are defined with respect to the presented architectural model. This allows to determine, in which way the considered approaches fail or succeed in handling the described challenges. Therefore, a conclusion on the need of programming models for mobile cyber-physical systems can be drawn.**

***Keywords*—cyber-physical systems; distribution; mobility; programming models; context awareness.**

I. Introduction

In the modern world, an increasing number of diverse computational units are interconnected. Especially in the context of the Internet of Things and Industry 4.0, this plays an important role. These devices communicate with each other in order to exchange data or coordinate their actions. An integration of sensors and actuators leads to the emergence of Cyber-Physical Systems (CPS), which consist of heterogeneous execution units, interacting with their physical environment. Sensors allow them to recognize the systems surroundings digitally. Based on this information, the devices control actuators to influence physical objects or phenomena. Therefore, a control loop is created, which incorporates the execution units (including sensors and actuators) as well as their physical environment.

CPS are used for a vast array of different tasks. Automated production lines [1], field fertilization by drones [2] and warehouse logistics management by robots [3] are just a few examples for this. In this context, considerations on mobility become increasingly important, as execution units (e.g., robots) and physical objects in their surroundings (e.g., goods being carried) may move.

In classic distributed systems, movements and locations of the execution units are hidden from the programmer through motion and location transparency, which are provided by the operating system or middleware. The deployment of these transparencies may become less beneficial, when the interactions of moving devices with their physical surrounds are considered. This makes maintaining distribution transparency more difficult. Positions and movements of single execution units and physical objects may have to be observed or even controlled by the programmer to obtain the intended behavior of the system. In this case, distribution transparency is still desired, as error-prone tasks like inter-device communication and coordination should be abstracted. This implies, that approaches have to be considered, which maintain distribution transparency, while providing support for motion and location awareness.

Programming models allow to take an abstract view on how these properties may be implemented. They describe the developers view on the system as well as its internal interactions. These interactions depend on the systems architecture. For that reason, we present an architectural model, which incorporates classic properties of CPS as well as the mobility of devices and physical events. This allows us to evaluate on which aspects of the system current programming models focus. On the basis of the architectural model, we define desired programming model properties to assess how present proposals tackle the mentioned challenges. We conduct this assessment through a Systematic Literature Review (SLR). Therefore, we are able to methodically inspect existing programming models with respect to the proposed architectural model and the desired programming model properties.

In Section II, the architectural model for mobile CPS is described. The desired programming model properties are presented in Section III. The methodology of the SLR is described in Section IV. In Section V, its results are analyzed and presented. Finally, a conclusion is drawn and topics for future work are proposed in Section VI.

II. ARCHITECTURAL MODEL

A layered architectural model for mobile CPS (see Figure 1) allows to view them in an abstract way. This is necessary, as the system encompasses the interaction of various fundamentally different entities, such as execution units, applications and physical phenomena.

Its lowest layer represents the execution units. Sensors allow them to continuously gather data about physical objects and phenomena in their proximity. Actuators enable them to influence their environment corresponding to the collected information. Heterogeneity is of utter importance in this context, as the devices possess different capabilities and therefore might have to cooperate to solve a given problem. Additionally, the gathered data of different execution units may correspond to the same observed physical object or phenomenon, but differs due to varying sensors being available on the physical nodes.

The environmental data layer abstracts from this heterogeneous view of the single execution unit. This is achieved by aggregating the gathered data based on its location and the corresponding physical phenomenon. Therefore, logical representations of multiple phenomena may be created, which leads to a global, more precise view on the physical world. This makes it possible to coordinate different devices to react to physical phenomena, even if they do not possess the capabilities to observe them.

The systems reaction to its observations is described in the application layer. It represents applications being executed on the different physical nodes. Those use the environmental data layer as a foundation for their calculations. The main goal of an application is to control the devices actuators to influence the environment. This is done according to the existing virtual image of the physical surroundings. Therefore, coordination and considerations on the heterogeneity of execution units are essential on this layer, as multiple different nodes might have to act synchronously to solve a common problem.

III. PROGRAMMING MODEL PROPERTIES

The described architectural model (see Section II) allows to view CPS in an abstract way. Programming models describe the interactions between the different architectural layers in an implementation-independent way. These models may be used as a basis for implementing a corresponding middleware or operating system and therefore, are well suited to be used as a first step towards further considerations.

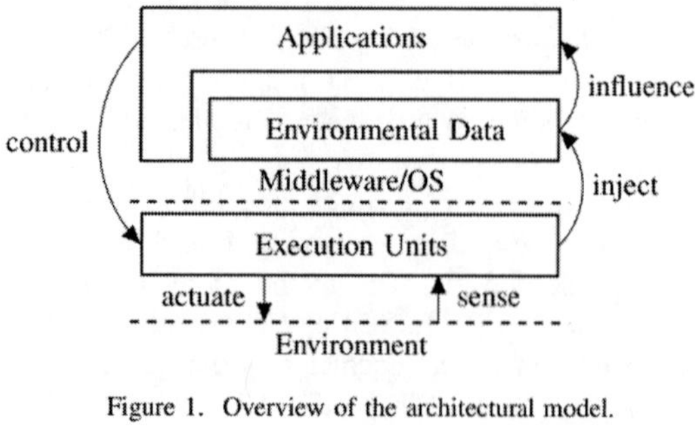

Figure 1. Overview of the architectural model.

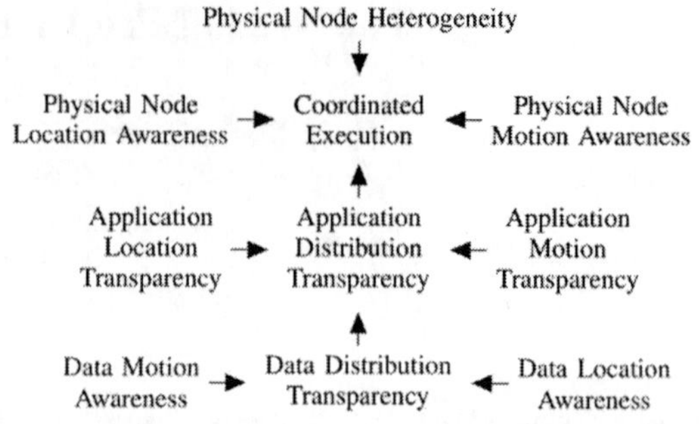

Figure 2. Relations of the relevant programming model properties.

As already stated in Section I, the focus of this work lies on mobility and distribution in CPS. Programming models may view both properties in different ways (i.e., through transparency or awareness). The provided architecture allows to consider them separately on the distinct layers of the system. Thus, the conflict of providing distribution transparency as well as location and motion awareness to the programmer (see Section I) can be circumvented.

When considering the discussed architecture, different kinds of motion have to be regarded for physical phenomena, execution units and applications. Through the implemented programming model, the programmer may not recognize the movement of some of these entities at all through motion transparency. Motion awareness contrasts this. It allows the developer to either observe the movement of these entities through passive motion awareness or to influence it through active motion awareness. When considering motion, location awareness has to be given, as motion is a change of location over time.

When regarding the different architectural layers, support of motion awareness (actively or passively) on the execution unit and environmental data layers has to be provided. This has to be considered to ensure correct interaction between possibly moving physical phenomena and execution units. On the application layer, motion and location transparency have to be deployed to provide distribution transparency. The programmer should not have to address execution units based on their locations and motion but rather on their properties and whether they are located close to physical phenomena of interest. This is achieved through allowing the developer to create one application, which is distributed to the corresponding nodes at run-time, depending on their capabilities and information gathered in the environmental data layer. Distribution transparency is required on the environmental data layer as well, as data has to be aggregated to a digital representation of the physical world. This allows all nodes to have an identical view on the observed entities. Therefore, a collective decision on which execution units tackle the corresponding tasks can be made. Location and motion awareness are necessary on this layer to differentiate between multiple different phenomena taking place simultaneously at different locations. Figure 2 illustrates the described programming model properties and their relationship to each other.

IV. Research Methodology

In this section, the approach for planning and conducting the SLR is presented. The SLR is based on the proposals of Kitchenham [4] as well as Biolchini, Mian, Natali and Travassos [5]. Its main goal is to inspect, whether there is a need for research on programming models for mobile CPS with respect to the presented challenges (see Section I). Therefore, contributions focusing on properties regarding distribution, location and motion awareness or transparency are examined as a first step. Figure 3 gives an overview of the research methodology. The need for a SLR is discussed in Section I. Additionally, a search for existing reviews on the presented topic is performed on *Google Scholar*. The search query encompasses keywords to identify SLRs on programming models for mobile distributed systems with regard to motion and location awareness as well as transparency.

None of the found articles are related to the presented topic. Therefore, the conduction of a SLR is needed. The research questions, defined in Table I, lay the foundation for finding, selecting and analyzing relevant contributions. They directly refer to the presented properties of programming models in correspondence to our architectural model (see Sections II and III). These research questions allow us to decide, whether the inspected approaches sufficiently tackle the described challenges. Thus, we can determine whether a need for research exists on programming models for mobile CPS.

A. Search Strategy

The selection of an initial set of papers is performed on basis of the following search strategy. Multiple trial searches are carried out on *Google Scholar* to identify, whether the results contain relevant articles. The research questions are taken as a basis for the keywords, used in the corresponding search string. If not enough relevant papers are included in the results, the search string is altered accordingly. Additionally, negative keywords are added to exclude articles regarding other domains, which may use identical technical terms with meanings differing from the presented definitions. The following search string is the final result of the trial searches and alterations:

("programming model" AND ("distributed computing" OR "distributed systems") AND ("mobility" OR "mobile systems") AND "computer science" -android -ios -"artificial intelligence" -"high performance computing" -multimedia -web -openmp -mpi -energy)

The initial set of articles, obtained through the use of this search string on *Google Scholar*, is used for the conduction of the SLR.

TABLE I
Research questions for performing the SLR.

ID	Research Question	Target
RQ 1	What are the used abstractions to provide distribution, location and/or motion transparency on the different architectural layers?	To get an overview over the used abstractions for choosing one or more of them for an incorporation into a new or existing programming model.
RQ 2	What approaches are used to provide location and/or motion awareness on the different architectural layers?	To get insight into the means to provide location and motion awareness for an incorporation into a new or existing programming model.
RQ 3	What kind of problems are solved by the programming models?	To identify, whether the solved problems are correlated to the challenges discussed in this work.

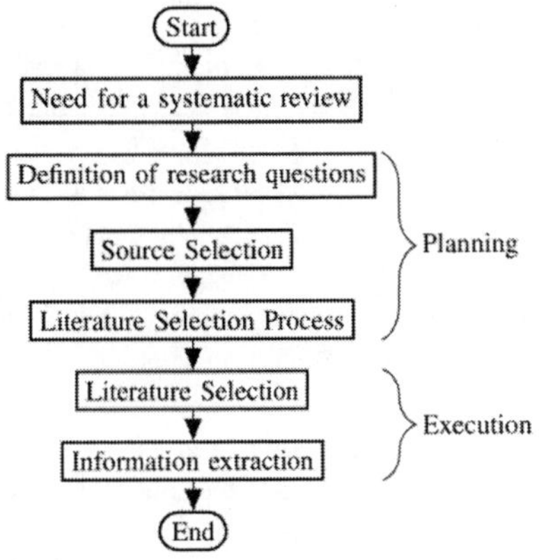

Figure 3. Approach for conducting the SLR [4], [5].

B. Review Protocol

The review protocol is constituted of the following aspects:

- *Google Scholar* is selected as a resource, as in a comparison with searches on *IEEE Xplore*, *Springer Link*, *ACM Digital Library* and *Science Direct*, *Google Scholar* provided the same results in addition to articles only being available in smaller digital libraries.
- The search method is based on a keyword search through the provided web search engine of *Google Scholar*.
- Papers focusing on programming models for mobile distributed systems constitute the population.
- Goal of the intervention is the comparison of existing programming models with respect to the presented architectural model and the desired programming model properties (see Sections II and III).

The article inclusion criteria are shown in Table II. They are directly connected to the research questions, presented in Table I. Articles are excluded, if they focus on optimization, energy efficiency, latency or other topics not directly related to the programming model, regarding distribution, location and motion.

C. Article Selection Procedure

The initial set of papers is filtered on the basis of the presented inclusion and exclusion criteria. First, all titles are read and it is decided, if the articles match the described domain (see Section I). For the remaining papers the abstract is read. If it is obvious, that the article matches the presented criteria, it is kept for the final set of papers. Otherwise, the

TABLE II
DEFINITION OF LITERATURE INCLUSION CRITERIA.

ID	Inclusion criteria
IC 1	The article describes the used abstractions of a programming model or middleware for mobile distributed systems.
IC 2	The article considers abstracting from or being aware of location.
IC 3	The article considers abstracting from or being aware of motion.
IC 4	The article considers distribution transparency.

introduction and conclusion are examined. If no clear decision can be deduced from the introduction and conclusion, the whole article is read and kept for or removed from the final list accordingly.

The initial set of papers is constituted of 452 articles, which is reduced by 236 through reading their titles and removing duplicates. The remaining results are reduced to a quantity of 19 articles by examining their abstracts and possibly their introductions and conclusions. Three more papers are removed by reading the whole text. Therefore, 16 articles remain in the final set of contributions to be reviewed.

D. Information Extraction

The information inclusion and exclusion criteria (see Table II) directly correspond to the presented research questions. Thus, the papers are examined for approaches to distribution transparency, location transparency and awareness, and motion transparency and awareness. This is done with respect to the presented architectural model (see Section II), as varying properties may be regarded on different architectural layers. Additionally, the discussed problems are inspected to decide in which way the contributions are related to the proposed challenges of our paper. The following paragraphs elaborate on the articles and the programming model properties.

Four proposals focus on the application layer. They mainly differ in their approach to providing distribution transparency. In [9] and [10], the developer takes the view of programming a given spatial region itself, instead of different nodes. In [9], this is achieved through creating an automaton for a static

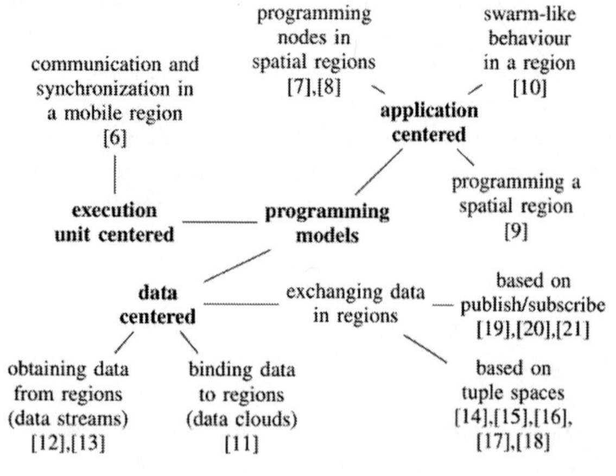

Figure 4. Categorization of the different research articles.

spatial region, which is emulated round-robin wise by the execution units, residing in it. Location awareness is provided on the application layer as well, as the programmer decides, in which spatial region a program executes. This implies, that location awareness is deployed on the execution unit level as well, as devices have to decide in which region they are situated. As they may move arbitrarily between regions (i.e., without control of the programmer), passive motion awareness is supported on this layer as well. In [10], swarm-like behavior in a static given region is employed, as one program is distributed over the corresponding physical nodes. Those perform calculations, based on their own state and the state of neighboring devices. Therefore, the execution of the different program instances converges. Distribution transparency and location awareness are provided on the application and execution unit layers for the same reasons as in [9]. Motion transparency is deployed on the application and execution unit layer, as movement of devices is not considered to be impactful. In [10], the environmental data layer is also regarded. Data is spreading from device to device through their neighborhood-based calculations. Therefore, distribution transparency, location transparency and motion transparency are maintained on this level. In [8] and [7], an application is created, which migrates between devices, based on their positions in space and their capabilities. Therefore, distribution transparency, location awareness and active motion awareness are provided on the application layer. On the execution unit layer active location awareness and passive motion awareness are deployed, as devices may move arbitrarily but have to exchange information about their positioning to decide, which computational unit executes the application.

Eleven approaches focus directly on the environmental data layer. In [13] and [12], the gathering of data from spatial regions is discussed. In [13], an application is executed distributively on spatially distributed execution units with the goal of aggregating data, situated on them. This implies the provision of distribution transparency on the application and environmental data layer. The information is accumulated depending on the positioning of devices. Therefore, location awareness is deployed on all layers. As positions of execution units are viewed as static information, motion transparency is maintained on every architectural level. In [12], an approach to represent data from spatially distributed devices as data streams is presented. As data is not aggregated, and distribution of it is maintained, no distribution transparency is provided on the environmental data layer. Location awareness is supported on the environmental data and the execution unit layers, as information is accessed based on its location and the point in time it was gathered. Since devices may move arbitrarily and the corresponding motion of information can be seen as a change of its location over time, passive motion awareness is maintained on both lower layers as well.

In [11], an approach to bind data to regions, instead of devices, is presented. Information corresponds to physical phenomena, which are sensed by surrounding execution units. The data is aggregated to create a more precise virtual image of the corresponding phenomena. Therefore, distribution transparency is maintained on the environmental data layer. Devices may move arbitrarily and spread the aggregated data according to the locations of the observed phenomena and agendas provided by the programmer. Therefore, location awareness and active motion awareness are deployed on the environmental data layer. The former is also provided on the execution unit level to enable the devices to decide, where physical phenomena are located. Passive motion awareness is maintained on this layer, as devices may move arbitrarily without the influence of the programmer.

Eight suggestions focus on the exchange of information inside spatial regions. They can be divided into approaches, based on the publish/subscribe paradigm or tuple spaces. In [20], [19] and [21], the publish/subscribe paradigm is extended to allow to constrain publishers and subscribers to only exchange data, if they are in a given proximity to each other. As no information about the location of information itself is given, location and motion transparency are supported on the environmental data layer. On the execution unit layer, location and passive motion awareness are deployed, as devices have to decide, whether they are in proximity to each other. Motion can be observed, but not influenced by the devices through the change of their locations and subscriptions to given topics.

Five approaches use tuple spaces to exchange information in spatial regions. In [14] and [15], each device hosts a tuple space and tuples may spread to other execution units based on given rules concerning directions and distances in space. As data is viewed in the form of single distributed tuples, spread across all devices, no distribution transparency is maintained on the environmental data layer. Location and active motion awareness are provided on this level, as the spread of information can be controlled, based on the positioning of devices. Therefore, location awareness is deployed on the execution

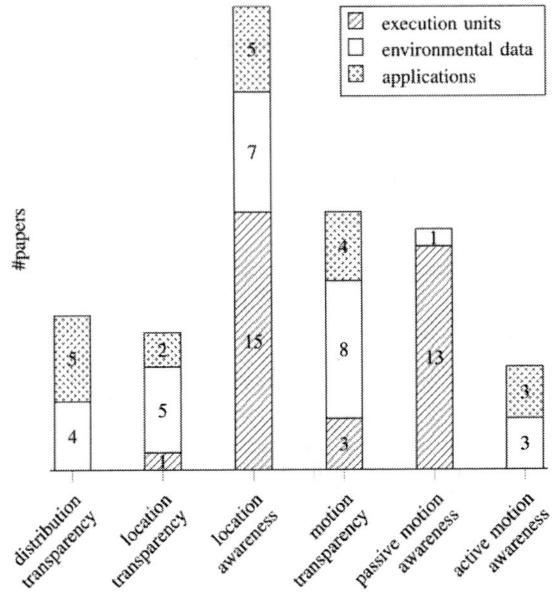

Figure 5. Discussed programming model properties in the reviewed papers.

unit layer as well. Additionally, passive motion awareness is provided, as execution units perceive their change of location without having influence on it. In [17], every device hosts a tuple space, similar to [14] and [15]. Additionally, tuples and reading operations are associated with geometric shapes. Only if the shape of the reading operation and the shape of the corresponding tuple intersect, information may be exchanged. Thus, location awareness is provided on the environmental data layer. Motion transparency is maintained on this level, as information may only be read from devices with the required relative positioning. Since devices may move in formation, the motion of data cannot be observed. On the execution unit layer, location and passive motion awareness are provided, as devices have to perceive their location in order to decide whether the geometric shapes of reading operations and tuples intersect. Additionally, they perceive their motion as a change of location, without having influence on it. In [18], tuple spaces are attached to logical mobile units, which may migrate between devices. Tuples may be exchanged between them, based on tuple space operation annotations regarding the logical units identities, regardless of their location. Therefore, location and motion transparency are provided on all layers. In [16], the developer creates multiple logical mobile units (i.e., agents), which perceive their environment through views. Each view contains data from other devices in a given radius around the current execution unit of the corresponding agent. Therefore, location and motion transparency are given on the application layer, as agents move with their devices or migrate between them arbitrarily and do not perceive their own location. On the environmental data layer distribution transparency is provided, as data from different devices is accessed similarly through the described views. Through the view constraints, regarding the positioning of devices, location awareness is maintained as well. Motion transparency is provided, as agents may migrate between devices, taking their views with them. Therefore, the set of data in its proximity changes, without actual information on whether the device moved, the agent migrated or other execution units or logical mobile units in its proximity moved.

One approach focuses directly on the execution unit layer. In [6], the programmer determines a region in space, whose extend and location may change, based on given functions. Inside the region devices may exchange messages. Programs are executed step-wise on the execution units. Whenever an according message is received, the execution of a step is triggered. Based on this, active motion awareness is provided on the application layer, as the programmer influences the movement of the region. Devices perceive their location to decide, whether they are located in a given region, hence location awareness is deployed on the execution unit layer. Additionally, passive motion transparency is provided, as execution units move arbitrarily between regions.

Figure 5 shows the final results of the information extraction. It illustrates the number of papers focusing on the given programming model properties for each architectural layer. The considered problems and which architectural level the proposal directly concentrates on are illustrated in Figure 4.

V. Analysis

As already described in Section IV-D, the reviewed programming models focus on different layers of the presented architectural model (see Section II). None of them is concerned with the interaction across all levels of the system, according to the given requirements (see Section III). Therefore, a composition of programming models or the creation of a new model is required. It is evident, that most approaches do not suite the presented needs, as they provide motion or location transparency on the execution unit or environmental data layers, or do not support distribution transparency on these layers.

On the execution unit layer *Autonomous Virtual Mobile Nodes* by Dolev, Gilbert, Schiller, Shvartsman and Welch [6] fulfills all requirements, as it supports location aware communication and synchronization between devices, residing in a mobile region. Therefore, it provides a first building block for further considerations on the higher layers. On the environmental data layer *Hovering Data Clouds* by Ebers et al. [11] fits the described needs. It provides distribution transparency through location aware data aggregation, regarding mobile physical events or phenomena. This directly corresponds to the described programming model properties for this layer. No programming model fulfills the requirements for the application layer, as they only support the programming of devices in static spatial regions. Therefore, if physical objects or phenomena leave the region, devices stop interacting with them according to the developers intentions. This implies, that alterations regarding mobile spatial regions have to be performed or a new model considering the application layer has to be created.

VI. Conclusion and Future Work

An architectural model for mobile CPS was presented in this paper. On its basis programming model properties regarding distribution, location and motion of physical phenomena, execution units and applications were defined. These considerations laid the foundation for the inspection of existing contributions, regarding the provision of the mentioned programming model properties. The examination of current approaches was performed through the conduction of an SLR.

The obtained results provide evidence, that existing programming models do not bridge the gap between providing distribution transparency to the programmer and supporting the motion and location aware execution of applications. Therefore, a need for research exists on how to incorporate these properties into one programming model.

As a next step, the results of this paper will be used to create an architecture in which further research will be applied. Topics for future work include considerations on the composition of existing models or the creation of a new programming model, as this may provide a more complete view on CPS to the developer. Further inspections on the formalization of such models are required to ensure the correct behavior of the system under any circumstances. In the context of CPS, the heterogeneity of devices in combination with concurrency is another subject for future work, as multiple different execution units might have to cooperate synchronously to interact with their physical environment to reach a common goal.

References

[1] G. Fragapane, D. Ivanov, M. Peron, F. Sgarbossa, and J. O. Strandhagen, "Increasing flexibility and productivity in Industry 4.0 production networks with autonomous mobile robots and smart intralogistics," *Ann. of Operations Res.*, pp. 1–19, 2020.

[2] P. Tripicchio, M. Satler, G. Dabisias, E. Ruffaldi, and C. A. Avizzano, "Towards smart farming and sustainable agriculture with drones," in *2015 Int. Conf. on Intell. Environments*, 2015, pp. 140–143.

[3] F. Basile, P. Chiacchio, and J. Coppola, "A cyber-physical view of automated warehouse systems," in *2016 IEEE Int. Conf. on Automat. Science and Eng. (CASE)*, 2016, pp. 407–412.

[4] B. Kitchenham, "Procedures for performing systematic reviews," Keele Univ., Tech. Rep. TR/SE-0401, 2004.

[5] J. Biolchini, P. G. Mian, A. C. C. Natali, and G. H. Travassos, "Systematic review in software engineering," COPPE/UFRJ PESC, Tech. Rep. RT-ES 679-05, 2005.

[6] S. Dolev, S. Gilbert, E. Schiller, A. A. Shvartsman, and J. Welch, "Autonomous virtual mobile nodes," in *Proc. of the 2005 Joint Workshop on Found. of Mobile Comput.*, ser. DIALM-POMC '05. ACM, 2005, pp. 62–69.

[7] C. Borcea, C. Intanagonwiwat, P. Kang, U. Kremer, and L. Iftode, "Spatial programming using smart messages: design and implementation," in *24th Int. Conf. on Distrib. Comput. Syst.*, 2004, pp. 690–699.

[8] Y. Ni, U. Kremer, and L. Iftode, "Spatial views: Space-aware programming for networks of embedded systems," in *Lang.s and Compilers for Parallel Comput.* Springer, 2004, pp. 258–272.

[9] S. Dolev, S. Gilbert, L. Lahiani, N. Lynch, and T. Nolte, "Virtual stationary automata for mobile networks," MIT CSAIL, Tech. Rep. MIT-LCS-TR-979, 2005.

[10] J. Beal and J. Bachrach, "Infrastructure for engineered emergence on sensor/actuator networks," in *IEEE Intell. Syst.*, vol. 21, 2006, pp. 10–19.

[11] S. Ebers, S. P. Fekete, S. Fischer, H. Hellbrück, B. Hendriks, and A. Wegener, "Hovering data clouds for organic computing," in *Organic Comput. — A Paradigm Shift for Complex Syst.*, 2011, pp. 221–234.

[12] S. Imai and C. A. Varela, "A programming model for spatio-temporal data streaming applications," in *Procedia Comput. Science*, 2012, pp. 1139–1148.

[13] R. Newton, G. Morrisett, and M. Welsh, "The regiment macroprogramming system," in *2007 6th Int. Symp. on Inf. Process. in Sensor Networks*, 2007, pp. 489–498.

[14] M. Mamei, F. Zambonelli, and L. Leonardi, "Tuples on the air: a middleware for context-aware computing in dynamic networks," in *23rd Int. Conf. on Distrib. Comput. Syst. Workshops, 2003. Proc..*, 2003, pp. 342–347.

[15] M. Viroli, D. Pianini, and J. Beal, "Linda in space-time: An adaptive coordination model for mobile ad-hoc environments," in *Coordination Models and Lang.* Springer, 2012, pp. 212–229.

[16] C. Julien and G.-C. Roman, "Egocentric context-aware programming in ad hoc mobile environments," in *Proc. of the 10th ACM SIGSOFT Symp. on Found.s of Softw. Eng.* ACM, 2002, pp. 21–30.

[17] J. Pauty, P. Couderc, M. Banatre, and Y. Berbers, "Geo-linda: a geometry aware distributed tuple space," in *21st Int. Conf. on Adv. Inf. Networking and Appl.s (AINA '07)*, 2007, pp. 370–377.

[18] A. Murphy, G. Picco, and G.-C. Roman, "LIME: a middleware for physical and logical mobility," in *Proc. 21st Int. Conf. on Distrib. Comput. Syst.*, 2001, pp. 524–533.

[19] P. T. Eugster, B. Garbinato, and A. Holzer, "Location-based publish/subscribe," in *Fourth IEEE Int. Symp. on Network Comput. and Appl.*, 2005, pp. 279–282.

[20] R. Meier and V. Cahill, "On event-based middleware for location-aware mobile applications," in *IEEE Trans. on Softw. Eng.*, vol. 36, 2010, pp. 409–430.

[21] L. Fiege, F. C. Gartner, O. Kasten, and A. Zeidler, "Supporting mobility in content-based publish/subscribe middleware," in *Middleware 2003.* Springer, 2003, pp. 103–122.

RefRec: Indoor Positioning Using a Camera Recording Floor Reflections of Lights

Shota Shimada
Graduate School of
Information Science and Technology
Hokkaido University
Sapporo, Japan
Email: shimadas@eis.hokudai.ac.jp

Hiromichi Hashizume
National Institute of Informatics
Tokyo, Japan
Email: has@nii.ac.jp

Masanori Sugimoto
Graduate School of
Information Science and Technology
Hokkaido University
Sapporo, Japan
Email: sugi@ist.hokudai.ac.jp

Abstract—**In recent years, there has been a growing interest in indoor positioning techniques using the ubiquitous infrastructure. This paper describes an indoor positioning method using light-emitting diode light reflecting from the floor and a smartphone camera recording it. Almost all traditional methods must detect the light source directly. However, there are some constraints to their usage since light sources cannot always be detected directly. Our proposal aims to solve this problem by estimating the position of a camera that does not face the light directly but records light reflected from the floor. The camera need not detect the ceiling lights directly from an image, unlike existing methods. Experimental results show that the proposal requires less than 1/100 the number of pixels for localization as do existing methods, and the 3-D position and attitude can be estimated within 0.27 m and 5.78 degrees at the 90th percentile in a 4.0 m square room.**

Keywords–Visible light positioning; Received signal strength; Angle of arrival.

I. INTRODUCTION

With the development of ubiquitous computing, there is great interest in Indoor Positioning and Indoor Navigation (IPIN) technology for mobile devices. In 2017, United States (US)$2,642 million in revenue from IPIN techniques was realized and this revenue is predicted to reach US$43,511 million by 2025 [1]. That is because IPIN has valuable applications in medical care, manufacturing, advertising, and sales, amongst others. In particular, the retail industry led the IPIN market in 2017 and predicted that demand such as improved customer searches, effective route planning, and optimized customer targeting would continue to increase. Customers usually do not prefer to obtain additional devices for IPIN, whereas many people have mobile phone devices.

From this background, many methods of the indoor positioning for mobile devices have been proposed. These utilize radio waves, infrared, sound, computer vision, visible lights, and others [2]. Among them, Visible Light Positioning (VLP), using a transmitter and receiver constructed by Light-Emitting Diode (LED) and camera or Photodiode (PD), has shown some promise for indoor positioning [3]. The receiver recognizes the light of the transmitters and then calculates its relative position to the transmitters. Compared with other methods such as those based on radio waves, VLP has three major advantages. First, VLP is efficient because LEDs can be used not only as lighting for humans but also as transmitters for positioning. Second, visible light does not penetrate objects, which reduces the multipath problem. Third, it is easier to install the VLP system because many buildings have the infrastructure for lighting.

Usually, LEDs should be modulated in high-frequency ranges to avoid humans sensing flickering, and to enable detection by the receiver. However, PDs used in Commercial Off-The-Shelf (COTS) mobile devices are not sensitive enough and their response rates are too slow for VLP. Therefore, we focus on a camera-based method using only a mobile device as a receiver.

Most of the existing camera-based methods use a large image for positioning because they need to detect multiple light sources installed at different places on a ceiling, directly from the image. It is computationally demanding, and some existing methods cannot calculate in real time using smartphones [4][5]. Also, it is too difficult to capture several LEDs into the image if the ceiling is low (it means a Loss of Signal: LOS). The user will therefore be forced to detect the LEDs by moving the camera. Some prior work also requires changing the camera to use a Complementary Metal Oxide Semiconductor (CMOS) image sensor that implements a rolling shutter. This feature enables multiple samplings in one image, but customers usually do not like the distortion of the image caused by the rolling shutter. However, there are developments to overcome this problem and this effect may disappear in the future [6].

In order to address these problems, we propose the VLP method RefRec, which does not find a light source directly but records reflected light on the floor. In our proposal, a camera captures light from the ceiling that is reflected by the floor and estimates the distance from the LED. No matter where the camera captures the floor reflection, the ceiling light will be reflected everywhere on the floor. The challenge is that reflections of multiple lights will be overlapped. To separate them, the frame rate of the camera and each frequency of LED light is determined by DC-biased Optical-Orthogonal Frequency Division Multiplexing (DCO-OFDM) [10]. Our experimental in a 4.0 m square room shows that our method requires $32 \times 32 \times 9$ pixels for self-positioning within 0.27 m and 5.78° at the 90th percentile. A comparison with existing methods is shown in Table I. The details are described in Section II.

Our contributions are summarized as follows:

TABLE I. COMPARISON WITH EXISTING VLP METHODS USING LED.

	Epsilon [7]	Luxapose [4]	PIXEL [8]	Rajagopal [5]	Nakazawa [9]	Our proposal
Accuracy of position	~0.4m	~0.1m	~0.3m	N/A	~0.1m	~0.27m
Accuracy of rotation	N/A	$\sim 3°$	N/A	N/A	N/A	$\sim 5.78°$
Method	Model	AoA	Polarized	PRR	Model	RSS
Coverage	5.0 m×8.0 m	1.0 m×1.0 m	2.4 m×1.8 m	3.9 m×8.0 m	1.0 m×2.4 m	4.0 m×4.0 m
Facing	Ceiling	Ceiling	Ceiling	Floor	Ceiling and floor	Floor
Distortion	No	Yes	No	Yes	Yes	No
Extra	PD	No	Filter	No	No	No
Number of LEDs	5	5	8	4	2	4
Resolution	N/A	7712×5360	120×160	1280×720	3280×2460 1472×1104	32×32×9

- The VLP method does not require large images and does not have rolling shutter distortion.
- The six-degrees-of-freedom mobile attitude estimation algorithm uses only modulated LEDs and a camera.
- Performance evaluation of the proposal was carried out by real-time positioning experiments.

We describe the challenges of prior works in Section II, our new method for six-degrees-of-freedom localization in Section III, the details of our prototype in Section IV, the experiments to demonstrate the advantages of our method in Section V, and the limitations of our proposal in Section VI. Our conclusion and future work are summarized in Section VII.

II. RELATED WORK

To explain the VLP method using PDs or cameras, some existing methods are selected, and their challenges are discussed.

A. *Visible light positioning using PDs*

Among the methods using PDs, Time of Arrival (ToA) [11], Time Difference of Arrival (TDoA) [12], Angle of Arrival (AoA) [13], and Received Signal Strength (RSS)-based [14] ones have been proposed. Our proposed method utilizes these previous RSS-based studies. Epsilon was the first indoor VLP designed in the academic community [7]. It detects the binary shift keying of the LED using the prototype device with the PD and derives the position by triangulation. Accuracies of 0.4 m, 0.7 m, and 0.8 m at the 90th percentile were achieved in three different office spaces. NALoc uses the same type of device as the ambient light sensor that is implemented in a smartphone. The results gave 90th-percentile errors of less than 0.35 m for the 2-D position, but the device was evaluated separately from the smartphone and not in a built-in setting [15].

B. *Visible light positioning using camera*

Camera-based methods allow geometrical separation of the light sources, allowing for more accurate positioning [16][17]. Luxapose can compute the position and posture of the smartphone by capturing ceiling lights directly with a camera [4]. The error is less than 10 cm and less than 3°. It uses 7712×5360 pixels in a WindowsPhone 8 smartphone camera as the receiver. The calculation requires a cloud server for high-quality image processing. PIXEL is a polarization-based localization method [8]. Only 120 × 160 pixels are required. It can be measured in several seconds with an accuracy of 0.4 m. However, a polarizing filter must be attached to the camera, so there is a risk of impairing the original image. Rajagopal's approach uses light reflected by the floor [5]. It is similar to our idea, but they focus on the rolling shutter distortion to receive an Identifier (ID) from the reflected light. Carriers up to 8 kHz can be received with a channel separation of 200 Hz. Tag information is transmitted by assigning ON and OFF bits to different frequencies. The data rate is 10 bps, and up to 29 light sources can be uniquely separated. Positioning accuracy was not discussed in the paper because the research aimed for the semantic positioning from differences in Packet Reception Rates (PRR). Further, because MATLAB was used for calculation, processing was not in real time. Nakazawa's method uses a dual-facing camera and calculates its own position by the relationship between ceiling light and reflected light on the floor. Large coverage and high accuracy are achieved using only two LEDs. This method also requires a large image so average processing time is 1.2 sec [9]. A comparison of conventional methods is summarized in Table I. Distortion means dose these methods require the rolling shutter distortion or not. Extra indicates an additional device for VLP.

III. SYSTEM DESCRIPTION

An overview of our system is shown in Figure 1. Our method is based on the following key approaches. RSS from the LED will decrease with the distance from the LED to the floor. More than two LEDs are mounted on the ceiling, which is parallel to the X–Y plane. The kth LED's known 3-D coordinate is (x_{L_k}, y_{L_k}, z_h). Each LED broadcasts a sinusoid wave with its own unique frequency. Modulated light from the LEDs is reflected by the floor, which is parallel to the X–Y plane where $Z = 0$. The camera of the mobile device captures any part of the floor P_{F_i}, then estimates its own position and attitude by means of three steps.

First, each distance $d_{i,k} = \sqrt{(x_{L_k} - x_{F_i})^2 + (y_{L_k} - y_{F_i})^2}$ is estimated. Second, the positions of several points P_{F_i} on the floor captured by the camera are estimated using $d_{i,k}$. Finally, the camera position (x, y, z) and attitude $(\theta_x, \theta_y, \theta_z)$ are estimated by optical AoA, using each P_{F_i}. The definition of attitude $(\theta_x, \theta_y, \theta_z)$ for a smartphone is shown in Figure 2a. The head of the smartphone points in the Y_c direction and the camera faces the floor at its initial status $(\theta_x, \theta_y, \theta_z) = (0, 0, 0)$. Also, we define 2-D coordinates in the image as shown in Figure 2b. The following sections provide details of the three steps.

A. *Distance between the light source and the photographed floor*

The first step is to find the distance $d_{i,k}$ from the intersection P_k of the perpendicular passing through the kth light source and the floor to the point P_{F_i} captured by the camera. The camera detects the intensity of the received signal from the

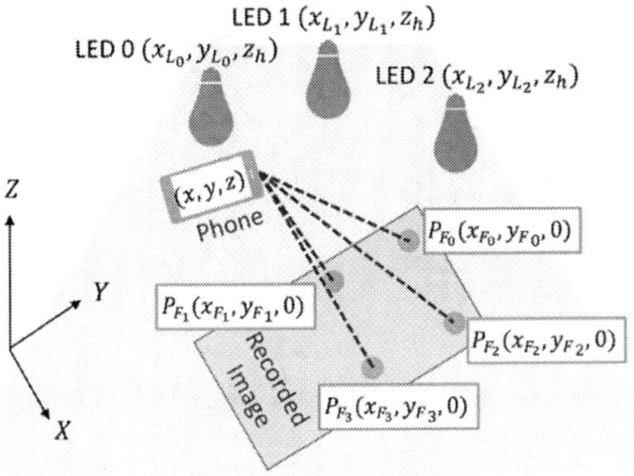

Figure 1. System overview.

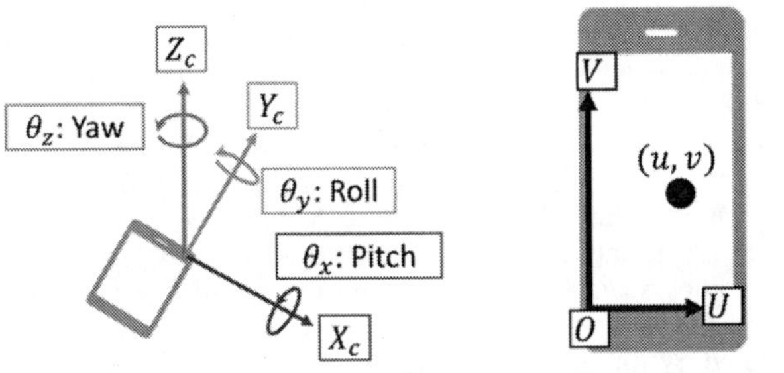

(a) Definition of attitude for a smartphone.

(b) Definition of 2-D coordinates in the image.

Figure 2. Definitions of attitude and 2-D coordinates for mobile positioning.

photographed image and substitutes it into the diffusion model of the LED reflected light. To reduce the influence of other light sources, the LED blinks a sinusoidal wave orthogonal in frequency to those of other light sources. We define $b_k(t)$, which includes a signal from the kth LED at time t, as follows:

$$b_k(t) = \sin(2\pi t(A_k f_s + m_k)) + \alpha, \quad (1)$$

where f_s is the basic signal frequency and A_k is a natural number so that the signal gets to a high enough frequency not to cause flickering; α is the direct current component, which makes $b_k(t)$ always a positive value; and m_k is a natural number that uniquely identifies the frequency for each LED.

Assuming that the camera frame rate is $f_c = f_s$, the shutter cycle is $T_c = 1/f_c$, the exposure time ratio is η, and the exposure time is ηT_c. By taking N images with the camera and separating the received light in the frequency domain, it is possible to extract the signal intensities of the unique frequencies. Therefore, the number of detectable LEDs is $N/2 - 1$, and $m_k < N/2$ should be satisfied as per the sampling theorem. By capturing $b_k(t)$ from the kth LED with a camera, the resulting brightness $I_{i,n}$ of the P_{F_i} on the nth image is an integral:

$$I_{i,n} = \sum_k \frac{2\pi X(d_{i,k})}{T_c} \int_0^{\eta T_c} b_k(t + \delta T_c + nT_c)dt. \quad (2)$$

where δ is the delay of the shutter timing with respect to the signal, and $X(d_{i,k})$ is the attenuation function that is determined by the distance and transfer efficiency from the kth LED as a transmitter to the receiver. Hence, our purpose is to calculate $d_{i,k}$ from the inverse function of $X(d_{i,k})$ using $I_{i,n}$.

Now, $B_{i,l}$ is obtained by the Fourier transform of the video stream $\mathbf{I}_i = (I_{i,0}, I_{i,1}, ..., I_{i,N-1})$:

$$B_{i,l} = \frac{1}{N} \sum_{n=0}^{N-1} I_{i,n} e^{\frac{-j2\pi nl}{N}}. \quad (3)$$

By assuming $\beta_{(m_k,k)}$ obtained by Fourier transform of $b_k(t)$, $B_{i,l}$ is shown as follows [18]:

$$B_{i,m_k} = \eta X(d_{i,k}) e^{j\pi f_k(2\delta+\eta)} \mathrm{sinc}\,(\pi f_k \eta)\, \beta_{(m_k,k)} \quad (4)$$

where $f_k = A_k f_s + m_k$. Thus, the unique frequency m_k can be extracted. Note that the amplitude spectrum $|\beta_{(m_k,k)}|$ is affected by η and sinc. Attenuation of magnitude affects the accuracy of positioning, so η must be set uniquely. Note that $X(d_{i,k})$ is the product of attenuation of the LED's signal and transfer efficiency. We assume the attenuation of the LED's signal is inversely proportional to the square of the distance and attenuates by the cosine of the radiation angle θ. However, it is difficult to model the attenuations theoretically because reflecting properties are very complicated in the real environment [19]. Our previous work showed attenuation on the floor can be approximated by a hyperbolic secant distribution [20]. Therefore,

$$X(d_{i,k}) = \frac{C_k}{e^{\frac{\pi}{2}\sigma d_{i,k}} + e^{-\frac{\pi}{2}\sigma d_{i,k}}}, \quad (5)$$

where σ is the radiation characteristic of the LED, and C_k is the transmission efficiency determined by the receiver sensitivity. Hence, the amplitude spectrum $|B_{i,m_k}|$ is shown as follows:

$$|B_{i,m_k}| = \eta X(d_{i,k}) \mathrm{sinc}\,(\pi f_k \eta)\, |\beta_{(m_k,k)}|. \quad (6)$$

Thus, $d_{i,k}$ can be calculated as

$$d_{i,k} = \frac{1}{\sigma} \cosh^{-1}\left(\frac{C'_k}{|B_{i,m_k}|}\right) \quad (7)$$

where $C'_k = \eta C_k \mathrm{sinc}\,(\pi f_k \eta)\, |\beta_{(m_k,k)}|$.

B. Position on the floor recorded by a camera

The second step is to obtain P_{F_i}-captured positions on the floor, using three or more $d_{i,k}$ estimated by the previous step. Now, we assume that three perpendiculars from the light sources pass through the floor at the points (x_{L_0}, y_{L_0}), (x_{L_1}, y_{L_1}), and (x_{L_2}, y_{L_2}) (see Figure 1). The estimated distances of these intersections to the point (x_{F_i}, y_{F_i}) are $d_{i,0}$, $d_{i,1}$, and $d_{i,2}$, respectively:

$$\begin{cases} \sqrt{(x_{F_i} - x_{L_0})^2 + (y_{F_i} - y_{L_0})^2} = d_{i,0} \\ \sqrt{(x_{F_i} - x_{L_1})^2 + (y_{F_i} - y_{L_1})^2} = d_{i,1} \\ \sqrt{(x_{F_i} - x_{L_2})^2 + (y_{F_i} - y_{L_2})^2} = d_{i,2} \end{cases} \quad (8)$$

By solving this, (x_{F_i}, y_{F_i}) can be calculated. When there are more than three LEDs installed in the building, it can be solved as an optimization problem:

$$\min \sum_k \left(\sqrt{(x_{F_i} - x_{L_k})^2 + (y_{F_i} - y_{L_k})^2} - d_{i,k}\right)^2. \quad (9)$$

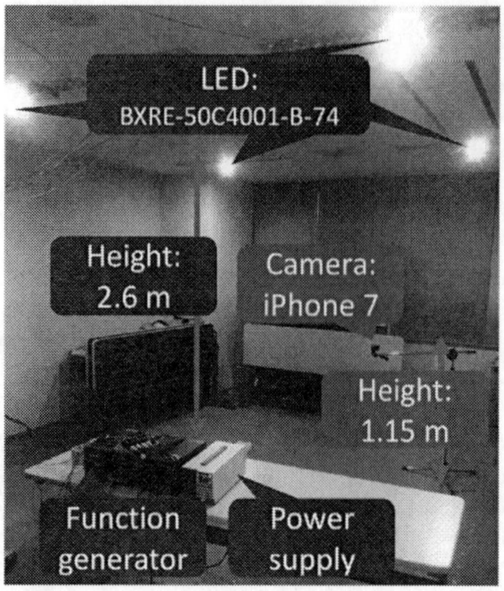

Figure 3. Positioning of the LEDs in the room and the camera settings.

C. Position and attitude of the camera

The last step is to estimate the position and attitude of the camera. These are calculated using the optical AoA method with the traditional camera matrix

$$sp = M[R\ \mathbf{t}]P, \tag{10}$$

where s means the scale coefficient, M denotes the intrinsic properties, and $[R\ \mathbf{t}]$ represents the extrinsic properties [21]. p is the 2-D image coordinates, and P defines the 3-D world coordinates as follows:

$$p = \begin{bmatrix} u_{I_0} & \cdots & u_{I_i} & \cdots \\ v_{I_0} & \cdots & v_{I_i} & \cdots \\ 1 & \cdots & 1 & \cdots \end{bmatrix} \tag{11}$$

$$P = \begin{bmatrix} x_{F_0} & \cdots & x_{F_i} & \cdots \\ y_{F_0} & \cdots & y_{F_i} & \cdots \\ 0 & \cdots & 0 & \cdots \\ 1 & \cdots & 1 & \cdots \end{bmatrix} \tag{12}$$

where the 3-D world coordinates (x_{F_i}, y_{F_i}) are captured by a camera as 2-D image coordinates (u_{I_0}, v_{I_0}) on the image. The camera position and rotation matrix $[R\ \mathbf{t}]$ is obtained by minimization of $||\mathbf{A}[R|\ \mathbf{t}]P - sp||_2$.

IV. Implementation Details

The prototype of RefRec using LEDs and a smartphone was implemented in our laboratory as shown in Figure 3. A floor made from a patternless nonglow mat was chosen because our prior work has shown that floor material might affect the result adversely [20].

A. LED transmitter

BXRE-50C4001-B-74-type LEDs from Bridgelux were used as the LED transmitter. Our proposal assumes that the light source is not an area or a line source, e.g., a flat panel or a bar light. Extending the experiments to including these sources remains to be done in future work. Four LEDs above the room were set as shown in Figure 3. The height of the ceiling is 2.6 m, coverage is 4.0 m square, LEDs 0, 1, 2, and 3 were set at $(1.0, 0.5, 2.6)$, $(1.0, 3.0, 2.6)$, $(3.2, 0.5, 2.6)$, and $(3.2, 3.0, 2.6)$ m. This setting was the same as the original built-in formation of fluorescent lights in this room. No other objects were placed in the room to evaluate the performance properly in an ideal environment. The signal parameters were set at $f_s = 50$, $\alpha = 1$, $A_k = 2$ (at any k), and $m_k = (1, 6, 13, 20)$. Hence, the LEDs were modulated at 101, 106, 113, and 120 Hz. These frequencies are higher than the 100 Hz modulation frequency for fluorescent lights in east Japan to ensure people do not experience any flickering. The transmitter represented any signal by the Pulse Density Modulation (PDM). A 5 V pulse signal from a function generator (NF Corporation WF-1948) was amplified to 34 V using a Metal-Oxide-Semiconductor Field-Effect Transistor (MOS-FET) K703 and a power supply. The frequency of the pulse signal was about 8 MHz. This was a prototype and the transmitter can be made cheaper and smaller by using a circuit similar to a dimmable off-the-shelf LED in our future experiments.

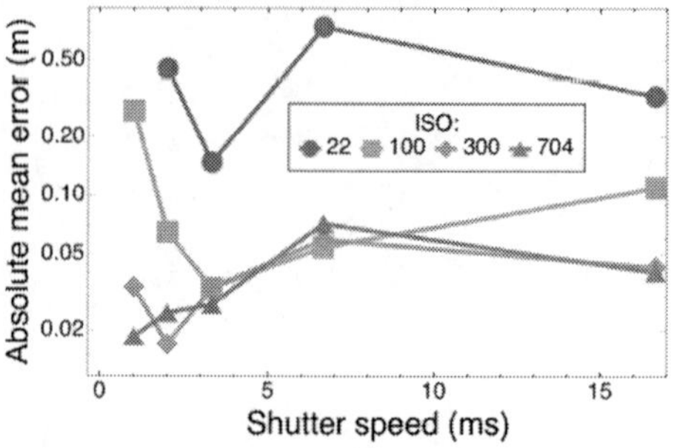

Figure 4. Absolute mean error of estimated distance for each ISO and shutter speed setting.

B. Camera receiver

An iPhone 7 was used as a receiver. Smartphones in recent years have generally higher-performance chipsets and cameras than the iPhone 7. Therefore, we believe that the experiments in this paper can be reproduced on other smartphones that users have. The frame rate $f_c = N = 50$ was set to avoid effects from other fluorescent lights. In east Japan, fluorescent lights are modulated by AC 100 Hz, so 50 fps is the orthogonal frequency, which will treat other fluorescent lights just as DC sources (the same as sunshine). The F value is fixed on f/1.8 in the case of the iPhone 7. The shutter speed and ISO sensitivity should be arbitrarily set so that the pixels are not saturated. The focus was fixed on the floor. Distortion of the image was calibrated using Zhang's method [22].

To reveal the relationship between the camera parameter and positioning accuracy, for each ISO and shutter speed setting, each distance was estimated by the following equation:

$$d_0 = \sqrt{(x_{L_0} - x_F)^2 + (y_{L_0} - y_F)^2}. \tag{13}$$

Note that (x_F, y_F) is the floor 2-D coordinates P_F captured by the principal point on the image. The iPhone 7 was fixed horizontally to a tripod 1.15 m above the floor and moved from $d_0 = 0$ m to $d_0 = 3.5$ m in 0.5 m increments. Each distance was estimated 100 times and absolute mean errors are shown in Figure 4. When the ISO value was set too low, the distance d_0 could not be estimated correctly. When the ISO value was set over 300, estimates at the centimeter level were achieved. We also found that shutter speeds should be shortened. However, shutter speeds that are too short make estimation difficult because the images become too dark. Hence, the settings of the camera are suggested that the ISO value is set at over 300, and the shutter speed is set at less than 1/300 sec. We subsequently set the shutter speed at 1/500 sec. and the ISO value at 500.

V. EVALUATION

In order to clarify the advantages and limitations of our proposal, the performance of RefRec was evaluated in our experiment.

A. Estimation of captured floor P_F positions

First, one P_F estimated by equation (9). The iPhone 7 does not support small resolution read-outs, so the resolution is set at 960×540 pixels, and used only 32×32 pixels around the principal point. Our previous work revealed this resolution to be smaller than that used in conventional methods and it enables real-time performance, while sufficient accuracy could be achieved for many applications [20]. The arrangement of the P_Fs are shown in Figure 5a as filled circles. The triangles indicate the LED positions on the ceiling. Since the parameters of equation (7) are affected by the individual differences of smartphone cameras and LEDs, calibration is performed before evaluation. Specifically, a camera was set with a tripod below LED 0 to receive a signal, and then updated the constant C'_k in equation (7) with $d_0 = 0$. The position of each P_F was estimated 100 times. All measurements were performed in real time on the smartphone. The mean positions of the P_Fs estimated by the camera are shown as non-filled circles in Figure 5a and the errors from the true P_F positions are shown as arrows. The error became larger outside the rectangular area with the coordinates of the four LEDs as vertices. Therefore, in order to measure a wider area, it is necessary to arrange more LEDs to increase the rectangular area. Since the LED beacons were set as square, the error should ideally be point symmetric with $(x, y) = (2.1, 1.75)$ as the origin coordinates. However, Figure 5a did not show symmetry because each LED has a slightly different feature. The cumulative distribution function of the estimated absolute errors are shown in Figure 5b. An estimation error of less than 0.42 m at the 90th percentile was achieved.

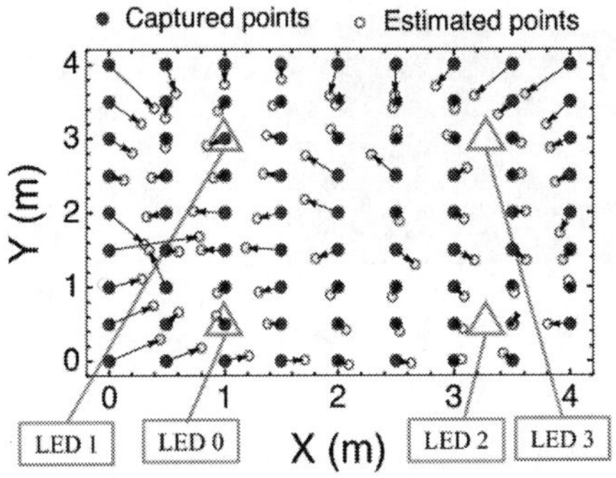

(a) LED arrangement, P_F measurement points, and estimated positions.

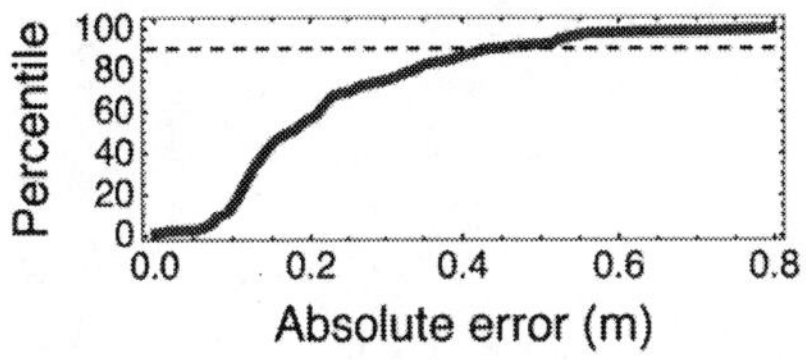

(b) CDF of absolute errors of estimated P_F positions.

Figure 5. LED arrangement and estimated errors of P_F positions.

B. Estimation of mobile device attitude using captured floor P_F positions

Next, nine P_{F_i} $(0 \leq i < 9)$ were estimated by one image stream. A resolution of 1920×1080 pixels was set. The principal point was $(u_c, v_c) = (524.86, 959.07)$. As Figure 6a shows, the 2-D image coordinates in p are $(u_{I_j}, v_{I_k}) = (300j + 200 - u_c, 300k + 200 - v_c)$ $(0 \leq i < 3, 0 \leq j < 3)$. A camera was set in the room with parameters $(x, y, z) = (1.0, 0.5, 1.15)$ and $(\theta_x, \theta_y, \theta_z) = (0, 0, \pi/4)$. Each P_F position was estimated 100 times in real time and the positions are shown in Figure 6b. The accuracy of the estimated azimuth θ_z for every combination of P_{F_i} was evaluated. The total number of P_{F_i}s is nine, so the total number of combinations of choosing more than one point from these is 502. This evaluation was processed off-line. The estimated absolute median error at each total number of P_{F_i}s used to calculate θ_z is shown in Figure 7a. When the number of P_{F_i}s used is two, the estimated errors are very different from which the P_{F_i}s are selected. The best 90th percentile absolute error was 6.15°, with the worst 90th percentile absolute error at 27.09°. When the baseline length was long (e.g., (u_{I_0}, v_{I_0}) and (u_{I_2}, v_{I_2})), the accuracy improved. On the contrary, the results for the cases with short baseline lengths (e.g., (u_{I_1}, v_{I_2}) and (u_{I_2}, v_{I_2})) were inaccurate. As the number of P_{F_i}s increased, the difference between combinations (standard deviation) decreased. When the number of P_{F_i}s used was eight, the estimated errors were similar, with the best 90th percentile absolute error of 3.25°, and the worst 90th percentile absolute error of 5.77°. In the next section, we discuss the use of all the P_{F_i}-captured positions.

The six-degrees-of-freedom mobile device attitude were estimated using nine obtained P_{F_i}s. The results are shown in Figure 7. The estimated 3-D coordinate positions of the smartphone (x, y, z) are shown in Figure 7b. The 90th percentile absolute errors of the x, y, and z coordinates are 0.2073 m, 0.1713 m, and 0.002464 m. Thus, an absolute error of less than 0.27 m in 3-D localization was achieved. x and y are more sensitive than z. The estimated mobile attitude (θ_x, θ_y) is shown in Figure 7c. The 90th-percentile attitude errors were less than 2.47° and 4.93° for the pitch and roll angles. The cumulative distribution function for the azimuth Z in Figure 7d shows a 90th percentile absolute error is less than 3.45°. The pitch and roll of the smartphone can also be obtained precisely using the Inertial Measurement Unit (IMU) [23]. However, it is difficult to estimate the azimuth using IMU because the magnetic field is unstable in the room. Our results show RefRec has potential for more mobile applications.

C. Angle precision of different attitude of the smartphone

To investigate the accuracy limitations of the smartphone's angle estimation, orientation errors from P_{F_i} were evaluated for each attitude of the smartphone. The pitch, roll, and yaw of the smartphone were changed by 10 degrees each, and its

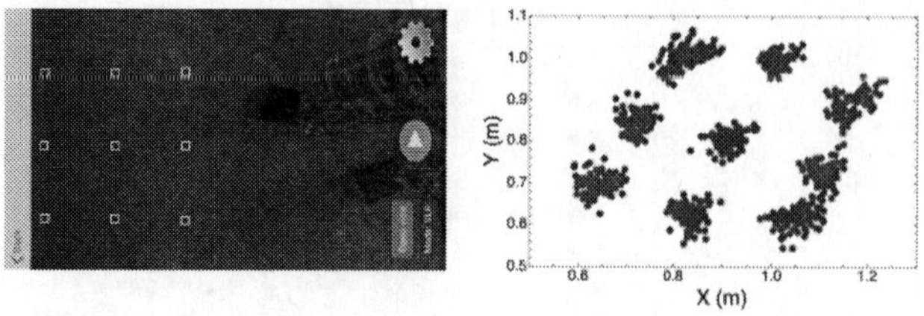

(a) Positions of p and the image captured by the smartphone.

(b) Estimated positions of nine P_{F_i}s picked up to calculate.

Figure 6. Arrangement of estimated P_{F_i}s and how many P_{F_i}s affect positioning error.

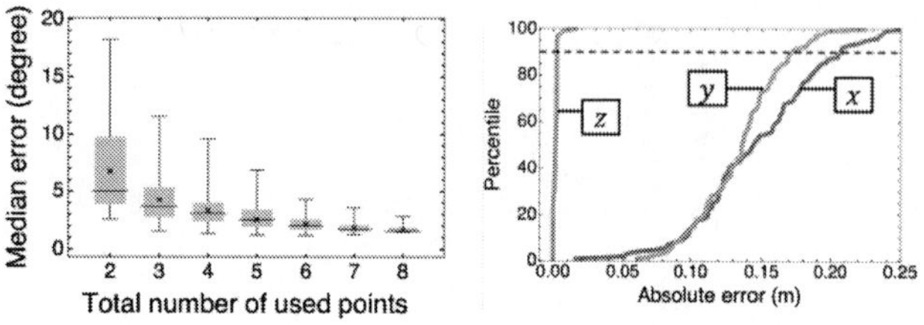

(a) Azimuth θ_z at each total number of points P_{F_i} used.

(b) 3-D coordinates of mobile position x, y, and z.

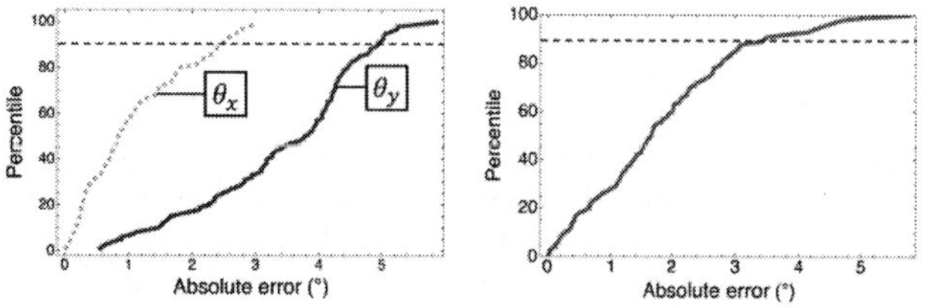

(c) Pitch θ_x and roll θ_y.

(d) Azimuth (yaw) θ_z.

Figure 7. CDF of estimated absolute errors about six degrees-of-freedom using nine P_{F_i}s.

attitude was estimated 100 times. Considering the use case of holding a smartphone, the roll, pitch, and yaw were limited to $-30°$ to $30°$, $0°$ to $30°$, and $0°$ to $90°$. Each 90th percentile absolute rotation error at each posture of the smartphone is shown in Figure 8. Means of 90th percentile absolute rotation error were $5.69°$, $5.78°$, and $3.96°$ for the roll, pitch, and yaw.

VI. Discussion

In this section, we discuss the limitations of our proposal and potential remaining future work.

A. Comparison of performance

A comparison of the performance of positioning is presented in Table I. Please note that each experimental environment differs in terms of LED installation spacing and measurement area size. Performance comparisons in the same condition are difficult to make because these differences have a significant impact on accuracy. For example, the best-accuracy Luxapose in Table I is difficult to localize in our experimental environment where the LED spacing is too wide to record multiple LEDs directly using smartphone camera.

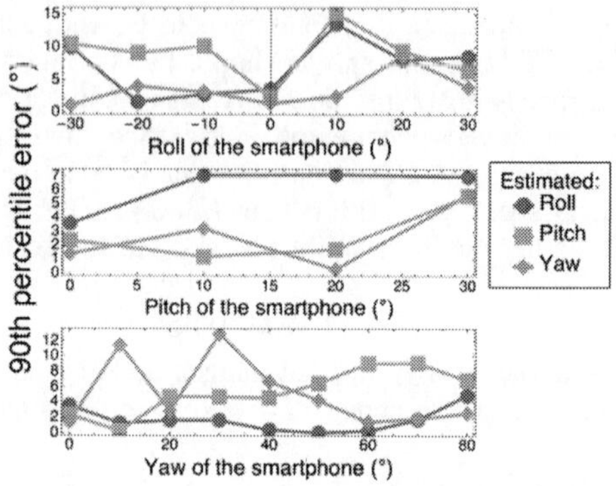

Figure 8. 90th percentile absolute rotation error at each posture of the smartphone.

B. Materials of transmitter and receiver

Changing the materials of the floor and the LEDs as transmitters may cause errors. In particular, LEDs with a Lambertian emission radiation characteristic are better. Our previous research showed that the difference of reflections resulting from different floor materials causes errors [20]. Future work must include investigating floors that consist of glowing materials or contain some patterns.

C. Attitude of smartphone

The attitude of the smartphone, especially its pitch and roll (tilt) attitude, may cause errors. We suggest that the smartphone should be held horizontally. We are of the opinion that this is easier to achieve than the existing method, which requires moving the mobile to seek the LEDs directly.

D. Power consumption

The camera consumes power using our positioning method. Approximately 300 mW will be consumed using an off-the-shelf camera [24]. If the user wants to navigate, it is necessary to continue activating the camera, so it consumes a considerable amount of power. However, because only a few pixels are required by our method, the power requirement can be reduced if the image sensor can activate only the necessary elements.

E. Solution in the real environment

In our experiments, nothing was placed in the measurement space in order to minimize signal changes. However, in a real environment there are many obstacles, such as objects or humans. The shadow of so-called ambient occlusion might be harmful to positioning. In the future, we will propose how to select an area that does not include shadows. We will also investigate influences and conduct experiments in larger spaces using, for example, 16 LEDs in a 10 m square room.

VII. Conclusion and Future Work

Visible light positioning for smartphones is regarded as a promising technique that is expanding the market in many industries. This paper describes an approach to avoid existing limitations, such as LOS, by using a camera recording light reflected by the floor. Our prototype showed 90th percentile 3-D localization and attitude estimation errors that were within

0.27 m and 5.78°. Our proposal has larger coverage and a smaller image requirement than conventional techniques. We also mention that some conditions may affect the positioning accuracy, such as the floor materials, radiation characteristics of the LED, and tilt of the smartphone, amongst others. A combination of our proposal and conventional techniques should reduce the limitations and improve accuracy. Future work will explore cases where, for example, more people hold their smartphones and move around, objects are placed on the floor to cause occlusion, more LEDs are used, and experimenting is done in a larger area.

ACKNOWLEDGMENT

This research was supported by Global Station for Big Data and CyberSecurity, a project of Global Institution for Collaborative Research and Education at Hokkaido University, JSPS KAKENHI Grant Number 19H04222, and Tateisi Science and Technology Foundation.

REFERENCES

[1] P. Lanjudkar, "Indoor Positioning and Indoor Navigation (IPIN) Market," https://www.alliedmarketresearch.com/indoor-positioning-and-indoor-navigation-ipin-market, 2018, [retrieved: Sep,2020].

[2] P. Davidson and R. Piché, "A survey of selected indoor positioning methods for smartphones," IEEE Communications Surveys & Tutorials, vol. 19, no. 2, 2016, pp. 1347–1370.

[3] S. D. Lausnay, L. D. Strycker, J. P. Goemaere, B. Nauwelaers, and N. Stevens, "A survey on multiple access visible light positioning," in Proc. 2016 IEEE Int. Conf. on Emerging Technologies and Innovative Business Practices for the Transformation of Societies, Port Louis, Mauritius, Aug 2016, pp. 38–42.

[4] Y.-S. Kuo, P. Pannuto, K.-J. Hsiao, and P. Dutta, "Luxapose: Indoor positioning with mobile phones and visible light," in Proc. 20th annual Int. Conf. Mobile Computing and Networking, Maui, Hawaii, 2014, pp. 447–458.

[5] N. Rajagopal, P. Lazik, and A. Rowe, "Visual light landmarks for mobile devices," in Proc. 13th Int. Symp. Information Processing in Sensor Networks, Berlin, Germany, 2014, pp. 249–260.

[6] Sony Semiconductor Solutions Corporation, "Sony Develops the Industry's First*1 3-Layer Stacked CMOS Image Sensor with DRAM for Smartphones," https://www.sony.net/SonyInfo/News/Press/201702/17-013E/, [retrieved: Sep,2020].

[7] L. Li, P. Hu, C. Peng, G. Shen, and F. Zhao, "Epsilon: A visible light based positioning system." in Proc. 11th USENIX Symp. Networked Systems Design and Implementation, vol. 14, Seattle, WA, United States, 2014, pp. 331–343.

[8] Z. Yang, Z. Wang, J. Zhang, C. Huang, and Q. Zhang, "Wearables can afford: Light-weight indoor positioning with visible light," in Proc. 13th Annual Int. Conf. Mobile Systems, Applications, and Services, New York, NY, United States, 2015, pp. 317–330.

[9] Y. Nakazawa et al., "Precise indoor localization method using dual-facing cameras on a smart device via visible light communication," IEICE Trans. Fundamentals of Electronics, Communications and Computer Sciences, vol. E100.A, no. 11, 2017, pp. 2295–2303.

[10] J. Armstrong and A. Lowery, "Power efficient optical ofdm," Electronics letters, vol. 42, no. 6, 2006, pp. 370–372.

[11] T. Q. Wang, Y. A. Sekercioglu, A. Neild, and J. Armstrong, "Position accuracy of time-of-arrival based ranging using visible light with application in indoor localization systems," Journal of Lightwave Technology, vol. 31, no. 20, 2013, pp. 3302–3308.

[12] S.-Y. Jung, S. Hann, and C.-S. Park, "Tdoa-based optical wireless indoor localization using led ceiling lamps," IEEE Trans. Consumer Electronics, vol. 57, no. 4, 2011.

[13] S.-H. Yang, H.-S. Kim, Y.-H. Son, and S.-K. Han, "Three-dimensional visible light indoor localization using aoa and rss with multiple optical receivers," Journal of Lightwave Technology, vol. 32, no. 14, 2014, pp. 2480–2485.

[14] H. Steendam, T. Q. Wang, and J. Armstrong, "Theoretical lower bound for indoor visible light positioning using received signal strength measurements and an aperture-based receiver," Journal of Lightwave Technology, vol. 35, no. 2, Jan 2017, pp. 309–319.

[15] L. Yang, Z. Wang, W. Wang, and Q. Zhang, "Naloc: Nonlinear ambient-light-sensor-based localization system," Proc. ACM on Interactive, Mobile, Wearable and Ubiquitous Technologies, vol. 2, no. 4, 2018, pp. 1–22.

[16] M. S. Rahman, M. M. Haque, and K.-D. Kim, "Indoor positioning by led visible light communication and image sensors," International Journal of Electrical and Computer Engineering, vol. 1, no. 2, 2011, p. 161.

[17] M. Yoshino, S. Haruyama, and M. Nakagawa, "High-accuracy positioning system using visible led lights and image sensor," in Proc. Radio and Wireless Symposium, Orlando, FL, United States, 2008, pp. 439–442.

[18] S. Shimada, T. Akiyama, H. Hashizume, and M. Sugimoto, "Ofdm visible light communication using off-the-shelf video camera," in Proc. 15th ACM Conf. Embedded Network Sensor Systems, Delft, Netherlands, 2017, p. 57.

[19] H. Zhang and F. Yang, "Push the limit of light-to-camera communication," IEEE Access, vol. 8, 2020, pp. 55 969–55 979.

[20] S. Shimada, H. Hashizume, and M. Sugimoto, "Indoor positioning using reflected light and a video camera," in Proc. 9th Int. Conf. Indoor Positioning and Indoor Navigation, Nantes, France, 2018, pp. 1–8.

[21] G. Bradski and A. Kaehler, Learning OpenCV: Computer vision with the OpenCV library. " O'Reilly Media, Inc.", 2008.

[22] Z. Zhang, "A flexible new technique for camera calibration," IEEE Trans. pattern analysis and machine intelligence, vol. 22, no. 11, 2000, pp. 1330–1334.

[23] P. Zhou, M. Li, and G. Shen, "Use it free: Instantly knowing your phone attitude," in Proc. 20th annual Int. Conf. Mobile Computing and Networking, Maui, Hawaii, 2014, pp. 605–616.

[24] R. LiKamWa, B. Priyantha, M. Philipose, L. Zhong, and P. Bahl, "Energy characterization and optimization of image sensing toward continuous mobile vision," in Proc. 11th annual Int. Conf. Mobile Systems, Applications, and Services, Taipei, Taiwan, 2013, pp. 69–82.